Endorsements for *Patrimonies*

In *Patrimonies*, George Kouvaros weaves a lyrical meditation through trails of history and remembrance: his own poignant, family-oriented path, and the chronicles keenly traced by visionary artists in the fields of film, video, photography and writing. How to honour the dead and preserve the significance of the past, while also clearing the ground and lighting the way ahead for coming generations? These essays form a global mosaic – wise, poetic and inviting.

Adrian Martin, author of *Mysteries of Cinema*

Have you ever noticed that there is a gap between the flame and its fuel? In this book George Kouvaros produces the 'type of quiet reckoning' that is necessary to notice how these small chasms can define our sense of the past and the future. The essays in this wonderful collection are written with the decorum that allows the author to move through and metamorphose with both his real and imagined ancestors.

Nikos Papastergiadis

Patrimonies

George Kouvaros

George Kouvaros is Professor of Film Studies in the School of the Arts and Media, UNSW. He is the author of numerous books, articles and book chapters on various aspects of film, photography and visual culture.

George Kouvaros

Patrimonies

Essays on Generational Thinking

First published in Australia in 2024
by Upswell Publishing
Perth, Western Australia
upswellpublishing.com

Upswell operates in the city of Perth, on ancient country of the Whadjuk people of the Noongar nation who remain the spiritual and cultural custodians of this beautiful land. We acknowledge their continuing connection to country and express gratitude to elders past and present for their strength and creativity…Always was, always will be, Aboriginal land.

This book is copyright. Apart from any fair dealing for the purpose of private study, research, criticism or review, as permitted under the *Copyright Act 1968*, no part may be reproduced by any process without written permission. Enquiries should be made to the publisher.

Copyright © 2024 George Kouvaros

The moral right of the author has been asserted.

ISBN: 978-0-645-87454-9

 A catalogue record for this book is available from the National Library of Australia

Cover design by Chil3, Fremantle
Typeset in Foundry Origin by Lasertype

Contents

No Longer and Not Yet   11

1   The Bouquet   17

2   Pacific Park   31

3   Moments of Choice   49

4   The Keys to the House   63

5   The Phantom's Call   75

6   'Together with Them We Are Also Alone'   89

7   'A Poor and Precious Secret'   103

8   'A Light from Before'   117

9   As If It Were for the Last Time   129

10   The Work of Mourning   145

Cities and the Dead   159

Coda   169

Notes   171

Acknowledgements   179

generations going,
generations gone

Derek Walcott, *Sainte Lucie*

'No Longer and Not Yet'

I

Collection of the author

Here it is, again: a photograph that since its taking has been carefully scrutinised, passed from one person to the next, buried among a pile of other photographs, rediscovered and, in more recent times, has taken its place alongside a range of objects used to recollect a past. From one angle, there is nothing unique about the photograph.

Spend time in the home of any family that arrived in Australia—or Great Britain, Germany, the United States, Canada, South Africa, for that matter—during the postwar period and you will find an almost identical image trailing the same history. Look at the faces of the adults in these photographs and you will see much the same mix of confusion and determination, expectation and anxiety. Harder to pin down, the faces of the children seem to shuttle between curiosity and indifference, as if they have yet to gauge how much of the fuss surrounding the taking of the photograph requires their cooperation and how much can be ignored. No one is being asked to smile, just to look straight ahead and allow the process to take its course.

The photograph we have before us belongs to the category of identity photographs: those images produced in their hundreds of thousands to accompany passport applications, visa documents and identity permits that, years after their production, resurface in photo albums and display cabinets. The contemporary appeal of these images is tied to their occasion: they show us the past not as something fixed or predetermined, but as marked by a sense of possibility. This is why, if we look closely at these images, noting their commonplace elements, we will hear a familiar tune, sung a little differently each time, whose purpose is to set the scene for a type of quiet reckoning. Photographs can be noisy places, full of voices that demand to be heard. The voices that accompany the photographs before us vary in tone and register: sometimes beseeching, often a little proud, nearly always rueful. Each is asking: Was it worth it? Did I make the right choice? What would have happened if I had made a different choice?

'What has made us human,' writes John Berger, 'what makes us what we are, is our awareness of past and future.' He writes this in a discussion of the photograph's ability to place this awareness in its proper context: our status as mortal beings, each moment moving closer to the point when the questions asked by these photographs will fall to the next generation either to ponder or ignore.

II

'The responsibility of the living to the dead is not simple,' claims Anne Carson. 'It is we who let them go, for we do not accompany them. It is we who hold them here—deny them their nothingness—by naming their names. Out of these two wrongs comes the writing of epitaphs.' These reflections help to clarify the questions at the heart of this book: how do we take from and give back to those lives that precede and shadow our own? How have their choices and actions left their mark on us?

In the first instance, this occurs through memory. The type of memory that I'm interested in coincides with an activity of writing that attains its urgency at a particular moment: the moment when one generation is passing—or has already passed—and another has yet to take its place. Hannah Arendt describes this as the moment of the 'no longer and not yet', an uncertain interval in which the continuity between past and future gives way to a form of thinking whose goal is not to determine the truth of a previous generation, but rather something more elusive: its legacy for us.

The essays in this book consider how generational thinking operates in different contexts. Read cumulatively, they employ a pattern of theme and variation whose purpose is to draw out an awareness of precariousness—of people, places and things *on the brink*. This is what gives the essays their sense of occasion as well as responsibility—to those who came before and those still to come.

III

To begin, we can return to the identity photograph and add some detail that only an insider can provide. The woman in the photograph is thirty-one. Arranged in front of her, according to age and height, are her three children, aged two, four and six. We can be definite about this because the photograph was taken during the process of gathering the documentation necessary to process their visa application for migration to Australia. Another photograph taken at the same time shows the woman's husband standing directly beside her and their three children. So, along with the age of the people in the photograph, we can add a date: 1966. Establishing a date is important, as it allows us to calculate the current ages of the figures in question. One other piece of information is worth including: the children's clothes and the floral-patterned dress worn by the woman were all made by her. On the visa application, her occupation is designated as 'housewife'. A more accurate designation would read: 'seamstress'. Like so many women of her generation who came of age in the villages and towns of southern Europe and the Mediterranean and whose schooling did not extend beyond a basic level, this is what she was taught to do and what she will do to supplement her husband's income, stitching together a range of garments, sometimes in overcrowded sweatshops, sometimes in her own home late into the night.

Looking at the photograph now, one is struck by the way in which the faces peer out from a background lacking contextual detail. This feeling of placelessness conjures the abstracting forces of officialdom, while bringing forward another element that must be written into our account of the picture. The woman's floral dress, the small girl's blouse, the boy's short-sleeved shirt, as well as the tunic worn by the eldest daughter: these items have been fashioned to convey an impression of respectability. But they are also evidence of a future that is being created stitch by stitch. The seamstress's labour projects the four figures gathered in the photograph past the uncertainties that define the present, towards a future when the sacrifices of migration will be judged worthwhile. Who lives in these futures? *We do*. It is our lives that have been plotted in advance.

Photographs are indeed noisy places. The source of the clamour can be traced to those passing details that belong to the moment of its taking: clothes, gestures, ways of carrying and presenting oneself. Even the feelings of uncertainty that mark the faces on show. None of this would resonate to the same extent if not for the presence of something else: an encroaching silence determined to assert its natural rights over the past. *Which of us really expects that their voice will continue to be heard once their time has elapsed?* The voices that emerge from the photographs, then, are really nothing other than our own voices, whose registers, intonations and breaks carry the imprint of voices that came before, that whispered to us while we slept and set our minds to look for so much of what was to follow. We are bound to be moved by these voices, for what they convey is that most mysterious and unreconcilable of things: our own voice at the moment when it reaches us as the property of someone else.

1
The Bouquet

I

They were the last couple standing: my father, still steady enough to rise from his seat without assistance; my mother, showing signs of recent health battles, but still looking younger than her years. The other couples in the reception room had resumed their seats, happy to applaud a marriage that had lasted this long. A marriage that had navigated the disappointments, slights and setbacks of starting again in a country that mixed its welcome with lingering suspicion. A marriage that, like many others at the time, was founded on the necessity of both parties taking a chance. They had made it. The marriage, I mean. But it had also made them. And now in this elegantly decorated reception room all the memories, large and small, that bound these two people had been lured out of their hiding places and were demanding their due. The object of their attention: the brightly coloured arrangement of flowers being handed to my mother by the young bride.

II

Those of us lucky enough to grow old with our parents enter into a particular type of complicity. We do not want anything from them. We do not want them to change or to show us something they haven't already shown. The only thing we want is perhaps the hardest thing of all for them to provide: an affirmation of their own happiness. If this is out of the question, then we will settle for some indication that their life has been well lived, and that by attending to its passing we might draw guidance about how to face our own demise.

In the case of my own parents, this involved a scene that I have retained in my memory and embellished with a range of emotions drawn from our life together. The event was the wedding of my cousin's youngest daughter. The ceremony was held in the same Greek Orthodox church in the suburbs of Newcastle that, over the years, has hosted the various weddings, baptisms, funerals and mnimosina that punctuate my family's history. Each time I attend one of these events I see people whose faces are so closely associated with this modest brick structure that I doubt I would be able to recognise them anywhere else. Mingling among these faces are the faces of uncles, aunts and family friends once part of this community, but now residing only in my memory.

The reception took place on the ground floor of one of the hotels overlooking the city's main beach. Seated at the table were my wife and daughter. Next to them, my two sisters and their children, my brother-in-law, as well as a first cousin from my father's side. Immediately to our right and closer to where the bridal party was stretched along a row of tables were my mother and father. Sharing their table was the bride's grandmother, my aunt, whose late husband sponsored our migration from Cyprus to Australia. The families of the bride and groom appeared to be evenly represented. The groom and his family were Maronites who lived in Sydney. The father was a mechanic and his son worked in IT. The warmth that pervaded the room had something to do with the fact that both the bride and groom were the children or grandchildren of migrants. We had gathered to celebrate their union as well as the achievements of those whose labour laid the foundations for this happy event.

The first hour or so was spent catching up with friends and family members, trying to confirm who was who, and putting names to faces that either bore a striking resemblance to someone else or had changed to the point of unrecognisability. From where I was sitting, I was able to do this while keeping one eye on the evening sky as it gradually darkened over the ocean. Having spent a good part of my childhood and adolescence working in the family shop, a stone's throw from where we were seated, it felt as if I had returned to a place that was deeply familiar, a place that knew both who I was and who I had become, and, despite the changes that had occurred, was able to view these two people as not very different, after all.

Just after the first course had been cleared, the master of ceremonies returned to preside over an important part of the schedule: the tossing of the bride's bouquet. The reason for bringing this forward, he explained, was to try something different. He began by asking all the married couples in the room to stand. He then asked couples that had been married less than five years to resume their seats. After they were seated, he asked those married less than ten years to sit. Then it was the turn of those married less than fifteen years ... With each upping of the years, the number of people still standing diminished, until the only couple left was my father and mother: my father smiling in that contained manner familiar to everyone in his family, my mother more animated and clearly enjoying the attention.

Despite the toll taken by a lifetime of walking back and forth behind a shop counter, they had aged well. The illnesses and infirmities that have come to dominate their lives had yet to diminish their spirits. Watching them, I felt a mixture of pride and reassurance. They stood there as my parents and as representatives of so many others who hadn't made it this far. But I also felt as if I was watching this scene from a point in the future. *Look closely*, a voice seemed to whisper. *Remember this moment. You will have cause to look back on what it shows.*

III

In his memoir *Patrimony*, the American author Philip Roth hears the same instruction. He describes watching his ailing father carefully manoeuvre his enfeebled body into the bathtub. Once this task has been accomplished, Roth takes a moment to observe the scene before him. 'Weakly at first, then more vigorously, he began to flex his knees and I could see the muscles working in his thin shanks. I looked at his penis. I don't believe I'd seen it since I was a small boy ... I looked at it intently, as though for the very first time, and waited on the thoughts. But there weren't any more, except my reminding myself to fix it in my memory for when he was dead. It might prevent him from becoming ethereally attenuated as the years went by ... *You must not forget anything*.' The devastation caused by the brain tumour that would eventually take his father's life spurs the demand to remember the details of a body that had once seemed impervious to life's ups and downs. Rendered vulnerable by illness, this enfeebled body must not only be looked at, but also remembered.

The difficulties associated with this task become apparent one afternoon, shortly after the biopsy that confirms the nature of the tumour pressing against his father's brain. During lunch at the author's home, his father rises from the table that has been set in the renovated summer room just off the kitchen and slowly makes his way up the stairs. When he fails to return, Roth decides to investigate. 'I smelled the shit halfway up the stairs to the second floor,' he recalls. 'When I got to his bathroom, the door was ajar, and on the floor of the corridor outside the bathroom were his dungarees and his undershorts. Standing inside the bathroom door was my father, completely naked, just out of the shower and dripping wet ... In a voice as forlorn as any I had ever heard, from him or anyone, he told me what it hadn't been difficult to surmise. "I beshat myself."' The scale of the mess is overwhelming. 'The bathroom looked as though some spiteful thug had left his calling card after having robbed the house ... "It's like writing a book," I thought—"I have no idea where to begin."' The association between the task of cleaning up his father's shit and the labour of writing is not metaphorical, he insists. The shit that his father had somehow managed to smear across every surface in the room in a valiant attempt to clean up his own mess is not a symbol of the patrimony he is endeavouring to memorialise. Rather, it is the patrimony itself—its most confronting, impossible-to-assimilate rendition.

Roth's account of his father's humiliation is shocking yet also deeply tender. His refusal to abide by the promise that he would keep this event private is a terrible betrayal. But it is also inextricably connected to his desire to understand the legacy of his father's fiercely contested life—its characteristic stubbornness and determination to never turn away from the realities of living. 'He taught me the vernacular,' Roth recalls of his father. 'He *was* the vernacular, unpoetic and expressive and point-blank, with all the vernacular's glaring limitations and all its durable force.'

The book concludes with an account of a dream that came to the author shortly after his father's death. In the dream, Herman Roth appears to his son dressed in a hooded white shroud. Just prior, the author had agonised over how to dress his father's body: in a shroud, as in the Jewish practice that had been used when Herman's own parents were buried, or in a suit, befitting his work history as a dedicated and successful New Jersey insurance man. In the dream, he is admonished for making the wrong choice. 'I should have been dressed in a suit. You did the wrong thing.' On waking, he realises that the rebuke was directed at the book that he had been writing during his father's illness. More broadly, it encapsulates the ongoing struggle to understand his father's legacy—what it demands of *him*. 'The dream was telling me that, if not in my books or in my life, at least in my dreams I would live perennially as his little son, with the conscience of a little son, just as he would remain alive there not only as my father but as *the* father, sitting in judgment on whatever I do. You must not forget anything.'

IV

In an address given on the occasion of receiving the New Jersey Historical Society award for *Patrimony*, Roth returns to the matter of his father's legacy. He describes his father's history as the first-born son of Eastern European Jewish immigrants who settled in Newark in the years between 1870 and 1910, a son who eventually fought his way up in the insurance business to become the manager of a mid-size New Jersey office, and who spent the best part of his life negotiating between the customs and traditions of his Yiddish-speaking parents and the demands of a fast-changing society. 'Assimilation is too weak a word, conveying too many negative connotations of deference and submissiveness and muzzling and proposing a story insufficiently gritty to describe this process of negotiation as it was conducted by my father and his like.' More apposite is the idea of 'a two-way convergence, something like the extraction and exchange of energy that is metabolism, a vigorous interchange in which Jews discovered America and America discovered Jews, a valuable cross-fertilization that produced an amalgam of characteristics and traits'. The citizen formed by this process was far from flawless and contained many points of friction, he admits. But, at its best, the convergence gave birth to 'a constructive mindset radiating vitality and intensity—a dense and lively matrix of feeling and response'.

Roth describes his father's experience of negotiating between allegiances as 'the quintessential American cultural battle that produces the classic family collisions'. But he also insists on those forces that made his father's version of this battle distinctive: 'The man or woman in the middle takes blows from both sides. First these children of the immigrant generation were made to feel inferior to the natives, ignorant in all sorts of social matters, graceless, crude, and worse, then they were made to feel obtuse and intellectually inferior to the children for whom they'd undergone their hardships. Yet how else to erase this gap but through the university?' The attainment of university education helped to overcome the social stigmas experienced by the previous generation—and it created a break between the world as it was lived by the father and the world that became available to the son. 'What began when my rabbinically trained grandfather went to work at the tail end of the nineteenth century in a Newark hat factory concluded when I received a master's degree in English literature at the University of Chicago virtually smack in the middle of the twentieth. In three generations, in about sixty years, in really no time at all, we had done it—we were hardly anything like what we were when we got here.'

Patrimony is about the obligations and uncertainties that accompany this process. Just as the author must remind himself not merely to look at, but also to remember the distinctive features of his father's ailing body, the book as a whole is engaged in an act of remembrance that is acutely conscious of its responsibilities as well as oversights. This awareness is evident in the dream in which he is admonished by his father for choosing the wrong burial dress. Even more clearly, it is at the heart of the injunction that appears more than once and functions as the book's closing statement: 'You must not forget anything.' These words can be read in two ways: as an attempt to give the final word to his father and as the invocation of a labour that one can neither realise nor abjure.

V

Watching my parents standing together in the reception room, the elaborately constructed bouquet carefully held in two hands by my mother, I was reminded of a photograph taken sixty years earlier outside the village church where they had just been married. My mother is in her rented wedding dress with the veil pushed back over her shoulders. In her hands is a small bunch of light-coloured flowers, much less grand than the bouquet presented to her at the wedding reception. Standing beside her, his shoulder not quite touching hers, my father is wearing a dark woollen three-piece suit that he bought when he was living and working in England, a few years earlier. I know this because, for a time in my twenties, I incorporated the jacket into my own wardrobe. Though it is long since abandoned, I can still

Collection of the author

feel the weight of the thick material pressing on my shoulders. On my father's head is one of the paired stefana that in the Greek Orthodox service symbolise the union of husband and wife. Unlike my mother, whose gaze is fixed on something to the left of frame, he is looking directly at the camera, the hint of a familiar smile on his lips.

In my eyes at least, the story told in this photograph is of two young people born in the same small village who, at different times and for quite different reasons, left its security for the promise of a life elsewhere. For my mother, this elsewhere was South Africa and an unwanted marriage that she spent four years trying to escape. For my father, it was England and life as a bachelor, trying his luck alongside other Cypriots, Indians, Pakistanis and Jamaicans who entered the country after the passing of the 1948 British Nationality Act, which granted citizenship rights to people born or naturalised in its colonies. My memory of the abandoned jacket is what remains of the story of his life at this time. The mishaps, adventures and moments of self-discovery that would have been central to this history have disappeared, snuffed out by his determination to forge a life free from the threat of impoverishment.

If I know a little more about my mother's experiences in South Africa it is not because she has spoken candidly about them. It is because of revelations that have come from others and the way in which, for the entirety of our life together, her emotions have set the tone for our interactions. This happens not in a selfish or hectoring way. It is simply how she maintains her availability to her children, an availability that allows us to read her responses as indicators not only of who she is now, but also who she was then. That she is able to make herself available in this manner is one of the mysteries that bind me to her.

Facilitated by the machinations of their respective families, the wedding was, I have no doubt, an opportunity to re-establish a sense of order in their lives. This is why their expressions in the photograph suggest an element of uncertainty about what they had gotten themselves into—*Who is this person? How will I know if this is one more mistake?*—as well as a willingness to accede to the demands of their new circumstances. If I look hard enough at the photograph, I can read some of the events that led them to this point, as well as the events to come: the struggle to find employment on an island riven by sectarian troubles, the failed migration to England, the return to Cyprus and, in between these events, the birth of their three children. I can also read the unresolved disagreements that surrounded the decision to set off once again, this time for Australia, and the difficult years immediately following our arrival. Alongside this, of course, are the many moments of happiness that make up a life together which, by any reasonable measure, can only be described as fortunate.

By superimposing two moments sixty years apart, the bridal bouquet awarded to my mother allows me to trace a connection between these events, a continuity forged in the face of everything that is determined to erase its possibility: geographic distance, the loss of tradition, illness, forgetting and the sheer happenstance that determines so much of our lives. But it also gestures to a time when the two figures whose lives embody the link between past and present are no longer. 'I shudder ... *over a catastrophe which has already occurred*,' writes Roland Barthes about an 1865 photograph of the manacled prisoner Lewis Payne. 'Whether or not the subject is already dead, every photograph is this catastrophe.'

Embedded in the ornate arrangement of the bouquet was a reminder of the inevitable passing away of what I hold dear, as well as the imperative to give this passing its due. The game devised by the master of ceremonies was a clever tribute to a generation whose labour had enabled the material comforts on show at the reception. It was also a moment when I heard the echo of that which I most dread.

VI

Driving to his father's house to relay the findings of the brain scans ordered by the neurologist, Roth misses the exit road that would have taken him directly to his destination and ends up on a part of the New Jersey highway running alongside the cemetery where his mother is buried. The unplanned visit to his mother's grave generates no sense of connection, no soothing remembrances: nothing, in other words, that might mitigate the fundamental fact of her absence. 'What cemeteries prove, at least to people like me, is not that the dead are present but that they are gone. They are gone and, as yet, we aren't.' This fundamental separation is counterposed in his ruminations by the dream in which his father admonishes him for choosing the wrong burial dress. The father who had found a place in his son's unconscious life has taken on a dual face: as the person whose shit the son has so diligently cleaned up and as the embodiment of something larger, a patrimony that he must answer to and find the means to speak for. Roth's achievement is to draw out the complex nature of this entwinement—between the living and the dead, between those who came before and those who must attempt to render an account.

In her collection of essays devoted to the crisis of tradition in modern life, Hannah Arendt refers to the attitude characteristic of Roman society to regard the past as a model and source of authority for the present: 'To educate, in the words of Polybius, was simply "to let you see that you are altogether worthy of your ancestors."' Arendt's book is fuelled by the question: what happens to tradition, to culture, to thinking when the figure of the ancestor has lost its authority and function as a model, when between the passing of an older generation and the emergence of a new there arises the possibility of an abyss? She acknowledges that there is nothing new in this situation. 'Basically we are always educating for a world that is or is becoming out of joint, for this is the basic human situation, in which the world is created by mortal hands to serve mortals for a limited time as home.' For Arendt, the imperative driving the attainment of education is something other than the desire for social advancement or the overcoming of social stigmas experienced by a previous generation. It involves the capacity to preserve and speak for a legacy—even, and perhaps especially, if we cannot be sure what this legacy asks of us.

'For the decline of the old, the birth of the new, is not necessarily an affair of continuity,' she adds in a different context. 'Between the generations, between those who for some reason or other still belong to the old and those who either feel the catastrophe in their very bones or have already grown up with it, the chain is broken and an "empty space," a kind of historical no man's land, comes to the surface.' They might not have known it, but this was the drama in which my parents' lives—as well as the lives of so many other first-generation migrants—were caught. In a good deal less than sixty years we were hardly anything like what we were when we arrived in Australia. But what I have come to realise is that this transformation did not commence when the five of us stepped off the ship that had docked in Circular Quay and made our way to Central Station to catch the train to

Newcastle, where my uncle was making a good living as the proprietor of the Brown Derby cafe. Long before this, the world that my parents had crammed into their three suitcases—along with the shoes and clothes, bath towels, photographs, a dinner set, and an assortment of knives and forks and cooking utensils that had seen better days even before their journey through the Suez Canal, down to Colombo, then on to Fremantle and, finally, Sydney—this world of taken-for-granted beliefs and expectations had, for my parents, lost its authority. It had acquired the status of a tradition that it fell to them to preserve—at the same time as they were participating in its demise.

Looking at their expressions in the photograph, I suspect that they too felt the catastrophe in their bones. But when I think of the life they made in Newcastle, it bears little resemblance to the 'empty space' that Arendt associates with the rupture between the decline of the old and the birth of the new. The historical no-man's-land in which we lived and worked and fought was filled with all sorts of ad-hoc arrangements, adaptations and uneasy accommodations. Closer to the mark is the 'pathos and blundering, anger and bruising, defiance, resistance, tears, and affronts' that Roth describes in his account of his father's upbringing. His reflections have allowed me to see this time in my family's history as part of a larger history. They have also helped me to reassess to *whom* all this was happening. Growing up, I believed that my sisters, cousins and I were the ones caught in the middle, experiencing the push–pull of different cultures and traditions. To an extent, we were. But no less so were our parents who, in their everyday lives and dealings with the realities of postwar Australian society, were far more exposed than their children. The experience of watching them and observing how they were treated made this obvious. It was easier to pretend that none of the slights registered and, by dint of their single-minded concern with achieving our social betterment, they were impervious to pressures and contradictions.

The difference was that my sisters, cousins and I had acquired a language to describe the experience—one provided by the education made possible by our parents' labour. The language that our parents used belonged to a world that we were unwilling or perhaps unable to recognise as our own. In much the same manner as described by Roth, access to education helped secure the process of social remaking and created a break between the generations. But built into this break were the means to give what had been left behind its due—not in a straightforward manner, but in the deeply ambivalent way in which writing links us to our forebears.

This is to say that, for the generation that grew up in the wake of migration and feels compelled to render its effects, writing is the patrimony. It is the arena where we confront head-on the inevitable entwinement of filiation and betrayal, where we negotiate what it means to occupy an interval between past and future. It is what we use to account for all that was gained, as well as a little of what was lost in the striving.

VII

For those of us who hear the injunction not to forget anything, this is what it means to accompany our parents into the realm of old age. The care that we show them is bound to that part of our selves that spans the uncertain space between who we once were and who we will become. Between the moment outside of a village church when two people familiar with the world outside the village find a way to reset their lives and the moment sixty years later in an elegantly decorated hotel reception room when the same two people take in the applause of friends and family acknowledging their achievement in having made it this far, a photograph asks something of its beholder: What do you see here? How much of this life will you remember and manage to pass on? How much will escape you and disappear? *You must not forget anything*. Writing is the patrimony and how we endeavour to make sense of the complicity it entails.

Now, while a patrimony may strike us on a deeply personal level, understanding it is never just an individual matter. It always involves an engagement with other lives and experiences. The capacity to forge these engagements is part of the patrimony bequeathed to me by my forebears. But it is also a consequence of my immersion in a world very different from the one experienced by my parents. For the entirety of my working life, I've been acutely conscious that when I commence work on a book or walk into a classroom, this opportunity has come about, in part, as a result of my own labours and choices, but in greater part as a result of the labours and choices of others. By this, I mean the willingness of a previous generation to leave the security of their homes and families so that opportunities and choices unavailable to them might one day be available to me. 'She spent all day selling milk and potatoes so that I could sit in a lecture hall and learn about Plato,' the French author Annie Ernaux recalls about the unequal exchange between her life studying at university and her mother's life in the small town of Yvetot. *A Woman's Story* is a belated attempt to understand the bond between herself and the world from which her parents emerged: to grasp what has been lost with her mother's death and what has been retained, in her.

We do not need to dispute the finality brought about by the passing of a loved one—the terrible feeling of *lessening*—to also believe that, so long as we can find the words to recall the people who have come before, the bond between who we once were and who we will become is never completely severed, and that the work of determining a patrimony remains unfinished. This is not to monumentalise the achievements of a previous generation. Nor is it to burden the work of remembrance. It is to hold these achievements in our hands as modestly as the bouquet clasped by my mother on the afternoon of the wedding reception. A memory of what has passed and what is still to come.

2
Pacific Park

> It is as if one can see where one has come from and where one is going ...
>
> Antigone Kefala, *Summer Visit*

I

How can we speak of places where families with limited means came and went, and made a living of sorts, places that act as meeting points between the old and the new, the long-established and the newly arrived, where each generation is given the opportunity to see itself as different from the previous one and hence able to break away? How can we describe the emotions that characterise these places, emotions that contain just enough volition to push a person out into the world in search of something better? How can we capture the manner in which these places remain behind, providing shelter when the noise of all this searching becomes too confusing, or the feeling of strangeness experienced when we return and discover that everything we thought we understood about these places was merely a product of our wants and needs? How can we turn this realisation into a story, not for ourselves, but for the people who brought us to these places, people whom we loved and spurned, and whose lives are bound to ours in ways too complex for us to understand?

II

Elevated view of Newcastle East. In Bruce Mackenzie, *Design with Landscape* (Sydney: Bruce Mackenzie Design, 2011).

Recently, I came across a photograph of an area of Newcastle that was taken from a position high in the building at the corner of Hunter and Pacific streets that was used as accommodation for nurses. Directly below the photographer's vantage point is Pacific Park, bounded, as it was in those days, on one side by the Royal Newcastle Hospital and on the other by the Hunter Street bus terminus. The left-hand side of the photograph is dominated by a cluster of terrace houses. Directly above them one can just discern the outlines of Fort Scratchley, perched on the headland overlooking Nobbys Beach. If we follow the line of the coast in the other direction, our gaze takes in the Ocean Baths, the Canoe Pool, located adjacent to the baths, and, finally, Newcastle Beach. The only thing that impedes our view of these landmarks is the Esplanade Hotel, whose rear windows look back towards the camera. The darkened windows and adjoining empty lot that has been turned into a makeshift carpark indicate that the photograph was taken during the long period of the Esplanade's dereliction, after it had ceased trading.

This is how I remember the hotel—not as functioning drinking hole for locals, but, like a number of other structures throughout the East

End of Newcastle, in a state of ruin, biding its time before the bulldozers arrived and completed its destruction. In the meantime, my friends and I would gather across the road from the derelict building to look up at its boarded doors and windows, and exchange stories about the terrible acts committed by our peers late at night in its abandoned rooms.

III

The photograph appears in a handsome hardcover book devoted to the career of Bruce Mackenzie, one of Australia's most renowned landscape architects. During the 1970s, Mackenzie made his reputation redesigning a number of Sydney's harbourside parks. Later, he oversaw the creation of the Joseph Banks Reserve on Botany Bay, the rebuilding of the Coogee Beach Plaza and the redesign of the Ku-ring-gai Bicentennial Park. In 1980 he was hired by the conservation-minded mayor of Newcastle, Joy Cummings, to lead the redesigning of Pacific Park. The project was part of a larger plan to rejuvenate an area of the city that had begun the twentieth century as a fashionable holiday destination for well-to-do families, but, in more recent times, was better known for the soot produced by the Zaara Street Power Station that would cover parked cars and cling to residents' washing.

The story that Mackenzie tells in his book concerns how this relatively small commission grew into a much larger exercise involving the demolition of existing structures, the closure of roads and the design of a barrier to protect the park's vegetation from oceanfront exposure. Inevitably, this expansion brought him into conflict with the city engineer, who was uncomfortable with the impact of the redesign on surrounding streets, bus lines and traffic flows. 'It seemed to me that this may have been perceived to be a step into engineering territory,' Mackenzie recalls, 'and in 1980, in Newcastle, some distance from Sydney, landscape architecture was still not that far removed from gardening.'

IV

Mackenzie illustrates his account of the project with detailed architectural drawings showing the proposed park and its integration with the nearby beach. He also includes colour photographs that document the fruition of his plans. By 1983, the Esplanade Hotel had been demolished. The termination of Hunter Street at Pacific Street and the relocation of the bus terminus allowed Pacific Park to incorporate the area across the road from the bus terminus. While Shortland Esplanade still separated the park from the beachfront, a new pedestrian underpass meant that park-goers were able to continue their journey to the beach unimpeded by traffic.

No doubt, Mackenzie's ambitious approach succeeded in beautifying the park and contributed to the transformation of the East End. But the relocation of the bus terminus and the closure of roads came at a cost to local businesses. With less passing traffic to draw on, one by one, the milk bars and cafes that lined the top of Hunter Street shut down. The next to go were the chemists, newsagents and other retailers. Eventually, even the grand old Newcastle Post Office closed down. Of course, other factors played a part in the area's decline. The increasing mobility of the population and the establishment of a number of large suburban shopping centres led to a decline in the number of people visiting the city to do their shopping. And as fewer and fewer people came to the city, the number of people who frequented Pacific Park also declined. For a number of years, the area around the park resembled a well-tended ghost town. It was only after the demolition of the Royal Newcastle Hospital in 2007, and the transformation of the nurses' accommodations and surrounding buildings into residential apartments, that the area showed signs of coming back to life.

V

Looking out from the windows of the nurses' accommodations, the photographer who captured the impressive vista probably had little idea of the changes to come. Because the photograph is uncredited, it is not possible to determine whether it was produced for the design submission or whether it was sourced by the architect from the city's archives. Its function is indicated by the presence of a white dotted line that designates the parameters of the proposed extension of the park. Within these parameters, three strategically placed rectangular labels containing the word 'Demolish' spell out what is soon to disappear. These labels reinforce the feeling of looking at a part of Newcastle that is gone for good.

When I look at the photograph of the old park, I see an area of the city captured at a particular time in its history as well as a place where an important part of my family's past unfolded. This was the part that occurred after our arrival in Australia from Cyprus, in 1966. By the time my parents purchased the lease on a kiosk on the promenade at Newcastle Beach they had been through a failed business, health problems and, in my mother's case, bouts of depression. Not long before, we had moved from living with my uncle's family to a small freestanding weatherboard house of our own in the suburb of Georgetown. The kiosk was the start of a new chapter, a chance for my parents to prove to themselves and their family members that the decision to migrate to Australia had been worth it. They purchased the lease in April of 1974. Barely a month later, in the early hours of 26 May, Newcastle was battered by a 172-kilometre-per-hour windstorm that generated huge swells along the coastline, causing extensive damage. Parts of the promenade at Newcastle Beach were destroyed, and the surging ocean flooded the kiosk. I remember watching my parents wading through the water and sea foam, quietly surveying the damage, wondering when their luck would change.

The piles of concrete rubble produced by the storm were in keeping with the building sites that pockmarked the nearby streets. In August of 1973, a master plan for the East End revealed that, as part of a proposed extension of Pacific Park, the surrounding buildings were to be demolished. The first to go were the takeaway businesses and cafes—the California Cafe, a Shipmates franchise selling doughnuts and soft-serve ice cream, a pinball parlour and, right next to the park, the impressive Kosciusko Cafe, which took up the bottom floors of two adjoining properties. The demolition of the Esplanade Hotel took much longer. After closing for business in 1973, it became the subject of a lengthy dispute between local residents and the city council, which was keen to push forward with the implementation of the master plan. By the time the building was demolished, on 24 November 1980, its dereliction had become an essential part of the beach's character.

Tyrrell House by Peter Sansom from the University of Newcastle Special Collections. Licensed under CC BY 4.0.

Thinking back, I was only ever half-aware of these changes. When we purchased the lease to the kiosk I was in the first year of high school. My younger sister was in the year below and my eldest sister in the year above. Walking past the building rubble and fenced-off areas, my mind was busy contemplating other things: namely, the injustice of being forced to spend my weekends and school holidays working in the kiosk. Prior to the redesign of the pavilion, the kiosk consisted of a single long counter that looked directly onto the beach. At one end were the fridges containing cans of soft drink. At the other end were the fryers used to cook an assortment of hot foods such as chips, fish pieces, potato scallops, Pluto Pups, Vienna steaks, Chiko Rolls, fish cakes, dim sims and doughnuts. In between were the chocolate bars, chewing gum, Life Savers, cigarettes, the freezers containing iceblocks and ice creams, the milkshake machines, potato crisps, women's sanitary products, surfboard wax, fly repellent and suntan lotion. If a product did not require lengthy preparation and there was some evidence of demand, my father was happy to add it to his stock. A year or two after he bought the lease, he installed two pinball machines. The racket of the metal ball bouncing off the bumpers and the clicking of the points tally blended with the background noise of customer orders as we traipsed back and forth along the counter.

On weekends and during the summer holidays, the rows of customers would be four or five deep. As well as family members, my father employed one or two others, often friends of the family. He would open the kiosk at seven-thirty in the morning and close late in the evening. I remember long stretches of days when my parents would return home at night smelling of the fat from the fryers, looking completely exhausted. The first thing that my father wanted to know was the weather forecast for the following day. He knew that, if the weather changed, a lot of the food that he had prepared would go to waste. For my sisters and me, another warm day meant another day working at the shop. We would watch the weather report hoping for some indication of an approaching cold front or the chance of showers. Nothing could make us happier than waking in the morning to the sound of rain. The first indication of a southerly wind change that would drop the temperature by four or five degrees and clear the beach of patrons was also celebrated as an opportunity to escape. Working at cross-purposes thus became an essential part of how the shop functioned.

The point I'm making is that the kiosk was more than just a business that kept my family clothed and fed. It was also a place where a new phase in my life began, one that required me to be much more conscious of the adult world—its routines, struggles and small-scale triumphs. Indeed, if I were to enlarge the photograph of Pacific Park, there is a good chance that among the group of people seated on the bench in front of the bus stop I would be able to identify a twelve or thirteen-year-old boy impatiently waiting for the bus to take him home. From the expression on the boy's face I would be able to read feelings of relief and guilt: relief that he was no longer traipsing up and down the counter, serving customers; guilt that, by heading home, he has left his parents in the lurch. This combination of competing emotions stays with the boy throughout his time at the bus stop and during the journey home, along Hunter Street, past Broadmeadow and right up to his stop, in front of the Sunnyside Hotel. Even when he is slumped on the couch, watching god-knows-what TV program, his mind is clouded by these competing feelings. It's only later, when the long summer evening has finally drawn to a close and the last of the remaining patrons have left the beach, that these feelings begin to dissipate and be replaced by trepidation, as he wonders what the expressions on his parents' faces will reveal about the extent of their exhaustion.

VI

Waiting at the bus stop, my greatest wish was to be elsewhere. When we first took over the kiosk, this meant being able to roam the streets with my friends. By the time I was fifteen, the wish to be elsewhere became entangled with the awkward feelings and transformations of adolescence. The kiosk made these feelings and transformations too public. As I grew older, I came to associate the empty lots and boarded-up buildings that surrounded Pacific Park with a broader malaise that was an undeniable part of the city at the time, and that arose from the loss of its industries, high levels of unemployment and entrenched bigotries.

My experience of these matters was through the day-to-day interactions with the people whose lives overlapped with mine in the kiosk. Not the suntanned families on the other side of the counter, whose relaxed demeanours were in contrast to the frantic back and forth movements of my family, but the council cleaners who arrived each morning to hose down the pavilion; the rival shopkeepers who we turned to when the kiosk ran out of change, on the understanding that we would do the same for them; the short-tempered delivery men who gingerly backed their trucks down the narrow ramp leading to the pavilion, rather than have to lug boxes of soft drinks or hessian sacks of potatoes down the steep stairs; the wheelchair-bound patients from the nearby hospital, each one of whom, according to my adolescent imagination, was suffering from some terminal disease that was also secretly working its way through my system; the hunched-over old Cypriot couple who came to the beach late in the evenings, talked to my parents loudly in Greek and tried to make themselves useful by sweeping the area in front of the counter—even the local hoodlums, who were in the years above me at high school, but spent their time propping up walls and inventing ever more ingenious ways to swipe the boxes of cigarettes from my father's storeroom. Most of the time, we got along. But in the end, it was these people, their routines and peculiarities, that I wanted gone, knowing full well that the only way for this to occur was for me to disappear.

VII

Of course, such acts of disappearance take time and, even if one is unaware of it, an element of planning. After finishing high school, I had a hazy understanding that attending university would offer a chance to study the subjects that interested me—primarily English, but also ancient history. The real goal, I think, was to buy myself more time. For what exactly, I was never sure. Newcastle University brought me into contact with an array of individuals from backgrounds vastly different from my own. By all the available evidence, these people were not only much smarter than I was, but also much better at understanding what was expected of them by their lecturers and tutors. Where I was prone to misjudge requirements and procedures, they were able to navigate these processes as if it was second nature. My failings did not stem from a lack of effort. It was simply that I had no model to call on that could show me how to turn effort into academic success.

The real benefit that I drew from attending university was the opportunity to cultivate a range of interests that compensated for my academic shortcomings: music, films, experimenting with various drugs, hastily arranged trips to Sydney to watch overseas bands ... and also photography. This involved not only taking pictures, but also learning how to develop the black-and-white negatives and make prints. This interest coincided with my first, short-lived, attempt to move out of home. I wish I could remember the circumstances that surrounded this event and how I explained it to my parents. But like so many other things at the time, it was something that I did with very little thought about its impact on others.

Along with the meagre rent, the main attraction of the dilapidated Federation-era house that I shared with three others was the size of the high-ceilinged bedrooms, which were perfectly suited to playing around with light and texture and staging moody portraits. These photographs helped to shape our identities in a city that we viewed as alternately hostile and accommodating. It was around this time that I also began to take photographs of my family. The ordinariness of these pictures reveals a desire to document something that, for the first time in my life, I was able to look at from a distance: my mother hanging out the washing; her, again, sitting at the sewing machine, adjusting a hemline; my father playing backgammon with a friend; him, again, behind the counter reading the newspaper. There are also photographs of my sisters and me, working at the kiosk. I say working, but what we are actually doing is reconstructing poses that belonged to a period of our lives that was not quite finished.

VIII

Collection of the author

The photograph that comes to mind was taken by my younger sister on a cool autumn day when, apart from my parents, just the two of us were working in the kiosk. It shows me at the far end of the counter, leaning on the freezer with my head cupped in my hands. The short haircut is of the time. So too is the exaggerated expression of boredom. The punchline is drawn from the juxtaposition of my bored expression in the bottom third of the picture and the hand-painted advertisement directly above, which shows a Pluto Pup covered in tomato sauce and a cone of vanilla ice cream. Between these two objects is a three-word exhortation that requires the reader to fill in the missing noun: 'TRY OUR *Delicious*'.

Three words, strung together without concern for grammatical requirements. But for my sister and me they were an irresistible opportunity. There was nothing cruel or malicious in our antics. We were simply using the occasion to distance ourselves from life in the kiosk. Distancing and rejecting are different things. But such distinctions were beyond my capacity to articulate—at least in a manner that might have reassured my parents. By this point, they had become accustomed to seeing us behave in this way. 'Paráxena paidiá' (Strange children), my mother would often say in response to our disparagement of some cultural protocol or refusal to mix with other Greek children. She didn't say this with bitterness. It was just another thing that she came to accept about the life that she and my father had created in Australia.

IX

By the end of second year, my interest in the courses I was studying had waned to the point where I was ready to abandon the degree. Too much was happening outside university for me to be able to focus on developing the skills required to improve my marks. Around this time, a number of my friends who were on the fringes of university life had moved to Sydney. When I discovered that I could complete the final year of my degree at a different university, I decided to join them. The only person in my family with whom I discussed this was my mother. In fact, we didn't discuss anything. I presented her with a heavily doctored account of my motives and intentions, which she dismissed out of hand. I had only recently moved back home. For her, moving to Sydney was evidence of my determination to turn my back on the home that she had worked so hard to create. *Strange children.*

The range of experiences that followed meant that I spent little time thinking about what was happening at the shop. But even before I left, I knew that the nature of the business had changed and the crowds that once frequented Newcastle Beach had relocated elsewhere. The redesigning of Pacific Park coincided with the long-delayed rebuilding of the beach pavilion that had been severely damaged by the terrible storm of 1974. The combination of the building works and road closures meant that parking was much easier to find at nearby Bar Beach or Dixon Park. The upside of this loss of trade was that I didn't need to worry about my parents' workload. My father must have been in his early fifties at this point and my mother a few years younger. Each day, they turned up to the kiosk, keeping the business going, while all around them the bulldozers and earthmoving equipment were bringing the revamp of Pacific Park to completion. If reaching fifty meant something to them, I couldn't say. My life and their shared life seemed to be proceeding along very different lines. As long as they remained in reasonable health, I could get on with the business of finding my own way in the world. The matter of their happiness—or grief—was beside the point.

X

In writing my account of these years, I need to avoid giving the impression of a definitive break. This was a time when almost nothing was definitive. Each move away from home and the emotional security of my family was matched by a move back. Things that seemed so important one day were, the next, liable to be cast aside. A chance encounter with a friend or a former housemate could have as much influence on my plans as any carefully considered goal. To put it plainly, I was riding my luck, convinced that, eventually, things would turn out for the best. Even if they didn't, there would still be enough time to set things right. This belief says a lot about the kind of person I was at the time, as well as the unspoken support provided by my family. Our lives *were* proceeding along very different lines. But what was never relinquished was my mother's belief that, regardless of my strange behaviour, she had the right to insist that, just as she made herself available to me, I had to make myself available to her.

It's not surprising, then, that, after completing the subjects necessary to qualify for my degree, I moved back to Newcastle. My goal was to save enough money to travel overseas. This is the time in Newcastle that I remember most fondly, working alongside my parents in the kiosk, staying back to help my father to clean the counter and wipe down the freezers and soft-serve machines in preparation for the next day, each week getting a little closer to my goal. When I could, I'd catch the train to Sydney and stay with my Australian girlfriend. Sometimes she would come to Newcastle. If I was lucky, my parents would let us stay in the same room. I remember being touched when my mother found a quiet moment one morning to tell me that my father thought this wasn't right. 'It's not fair for her family,' she said.

Did he really think this—or was she putting words in his mouth? As with nearly everything about my father's thoughts and feelings, I had to take her word for it.

XI

I was overseas for just under a year, travelling across Europe, spending time in Cyprus with my grandparents and living with friends in London. When I returned to Australia at the start of 1984, I moved back to Sydney. By this stage my father was considering selling the lease to the kiosk. The strain of working two jobs—the shop during the day and as a cleaner at Newcastle Railway Station at night—had taken its toll on his health. After he sold the lease, my parents returned to Cyprus for an extended holiday with my sisters. It was during this time that my mother's dream of returning permanently came closest to fruition. Everything hinged on her ability to line up suitable husbands for my sisters. If they remained in Cyprus, it would make sense for the rest of us to also remain. She had seen how this unfolded with other families, and with a little luck it might also happen to us.

Unfortunately for her, this proved to be just a pipedream. Having spent nearly their whole lives in Australia, my sisters found the realities of Cypriot life too difficult to align with their expectations for the future. When my parents did eventually leave Newcastle, it was not for Cyprus. Instead, they followed their children to Sydney. They bought the lease on a takeaway in Bankstown and rented an apartment nearby. After a year, it became clear that the business wasn't viable. Luckily, they managed to offload the lease before it had a catastrophic effect on their finances. They came close to buying a number of other food businesses in Sydney, without ever going through with the purchase.

In the end, they settled on a small fish-and-chip shop, just on the Sydney side of the Swansea Bridge, south of Newcastle. There was no four-foot-high Pluto Pup or vanilla ice-cream cone, just a brightly coloured sign on the front window: 'Jim and Pat's Fish 'n' Chips!' They held onto this business for eleven years, working the same seven-days-a-week schedule that they had at the kiosk. My sisters and I married and, soon after, started families of our own. It was around this time that my life and the lives of my parents became more intertwined. Although she still lived in Newcastle, every fortnight my mother would drive to Sydney to help with childcare. In turn, we tried to get to Newcastle as often as possible.

XII

Reading over my account of some of the things that happened after we sold the kiosk, I'm conscious of having jumped over major milestones. Leaving home for good, getting a job, meeting my partner, getting married, starting a family ... All these events have blended into one undifferentiated period that could be termed my early adulthood, a period that has none of the coherence of the preceding period, when the routines of life in the kiosk seemed to hold things together.

What I remember most clearly from the time when my parents had the shop in Swansea are the rituals that managed to bind the different parts of my life. Simple matters like stopping at the shop on our way into Newcastle and sitting down at one of the tables with my parents to share a meal. I remember the smell of the tomato sauce that would leave a trail across the side of my daughter's face and the joy that this sight brought to my parents. After finishing the meal, we would continue the journey into Newcastle and wait at my parents' house until they closed the shop. Once I had unpacked the car and set up my daughter's cot in one of the bedrooms, I would wander around the house with no real purpose, opening drawers and pulling things out of the bookshelves, never failing to be surprised at what, of all the paraphernalia of our childhood, my mother had decided to keep. I would do this with one eye on the clock. As the early evening passed into night, my thoughts would turn to the shop in Swansea. Was it just my parents working—or did they have someone to help them with the evening rush?

Increasingly, I'd find myself recalling those evenings in Newcastle when I had manufactured an excuse to escape from the kiosk and would wait at home for them to return. Looking at the awkward high-school photographs that my mother had framed and placed on her sideboard, I'd remember the feelings of relief and guilt, and how much I wanted to escape the routines that governed my life working in the kiosk. And not just the routines, but also the people with which they were associated. This had happened. But as I waited for my parents to return, I knew that a part of who I was as a person, perhaps even a fundamental part, was still waiting at the bus stop at Pacific Park, unsure of whether to head back to the kiosk or to press on with the escape, regardless.

XIII

Since my parents sold the shop in Swansea and moved back to Sydney, I visit Newcastle less and less. When I do go, it's usually for a wedding or the funeral of a relative or family friend. On these occasions, I try to stay somewhere that is walking distance from Pacific Park. The area near the park is now dominated by boutique apartments and cafes that, on weekends, are full of people crammed together, enjoying the views to the beach. Everything about the location and the people I pass on my walks confirms that the memories I associate with this place belong to another time. The proper thing to do is to consign these memories to the past. What stops me from doing this is more complicated than nostalgia. It is to do with the intensity that characterises those periods in our lives when something changes, irrevocably: when we move from one set of determining conditions and expectations to something very different. The trip back is about the afterlife of what was left behind—as well as the echo of messages that went unheeded at the time.

XIV

Near the end of Italo Calvino's *Invisible Cities*, the emperor Kublai Khan tells Marco Polo of the futility of realising that, for all the magnificence of the cities spread across his vast empire, the final landing place can only ever be the 'infernal city'. Polo encourages the emperor to see the inferno not as what lies ahead, but as what is already all around us, 'the inferno where we live every day, that we form by being together'. He then outlines two ways in which a person might escape the inferno's suffering. The first is to accept the inferno and 'become such a part of it that you can no longer see it'. The second is far more challenging and not without risks: 'Seek and learn to recognize who and what, in the midst of the inferno, are not inferno, then make them endure, give them space.'

I began this story believing that it would be about a particular place. I realise that it changed into a story about the people who brought me to this place. It doesn't take much to see that these are two parts of the one story, a story about the memories triggered by the photograph of Pacific Park. The shape and model of the buses that approach the terminus, the pose of the male commuter caught mid-stride as he walks purposefully towards the door of the first bus, the rear entrances of the rundown terrace houses across the street that look out onto empty lots made dusty and uneven by the buried rubble of what has been demolished, the darkened windows of the derelict Esplanade Hotel, the design of the park itself which, when seen from above, resembles an eye gazing up to the sky. These details show me the world of my past at its most particular. But they also remind me of everything that was abandoned in the striving.

This, too, is part of the photograph of Pacific Park, the part that is connected to the memories that I have of the people who inhabited this area of Newcastle, with their resentments, habits and struggles. Most of all, it is that part of the photograph which speaks to me of my parents' labour, their traipsing up and down the counter, day in and day out, and the toll that this took on their bodies and minds. They never made it big. But they did make certain things possible that weren't possible before: education, social mobility, as well as a type of distance whereby a child of theirs could look at the world in which he was immersed, its possibilities and choices, and obtain a degree of pleasure in willing it all to disappear. Recollection and oblivion. Home and the loss of home. Pacific Park is where these forces run together. But it is also the sound generated by two words, whispered one after the other—*Pacific Park, Pacific Park*. Like the jingle of a desk clerk's bell, it awakens me to where I've come from, and where I will be heading.

3
Moments of Choice

Collection of the author

I

For many years after we arrived in Australia, the most important connection to our former home in Cyprus was my mother's photo album. Most of the images in the album are of my mother's family: her parents, siblings, aunts and uncles. Every now and then, a page is devoted to my father's relatives. There is nothing wrong in admitting that these figures were supporting players; their role was to fill in the background, rather than to play a determining part in the story. Guided by my mother's prompts, I used these images to draw together some of the threads that made up our family history, at a time when my knowledge of this history had been foreshortened by the dislocation of starting over in a new country. Here is a photo of a handsome uncle who went to London to study chemistry. Next to him is his serious-looking older brother, who was both a high-ranking officer in the colonial police force and a clandestine member of EOKA during the time of the troubles.[1] Nearby is a portrait of one of my mother's cousins dressed in her neatly ironed high-school uniform. She is standing next to a side table on which rests a vase filled with freshly picked cyclamens. The photograph was taken just before the botched operation on her left eye that left her partially blind. Gazing directly at the camera with a mixture of pride and youthful embarrassment, her expression betrays no hint of this fate.

The centrepiece of the album is a series of postcard-sized wedding photographs and studio portraits featuring my mother's sisters and brothers. Glorious in their white dresses and dark suits, these figures embodied a past whose primary demand on my consciousness was a call to remember and resist the forces of amnesia that were propelling my life forward.

---

1   EOKA (Ethniki Organosis Kyprion Agoniston) was a nationalist paramilitary organisation that between 1957 and 1959 was responsible for a spate of bombings and assassinations which targeted the institutions of British colonial administration, as well as individuals and political groups seen to be opposed to the goal of unifying Cyprus with Greece. Britain responded by hanging convicted perpetrators, and instituting repressive measures against individuals and villages suspected of supporting EOKA's activities.

Collection of the author

Near the back of the album the highly posed black-and-white images are replaced by colour snapshots, most of which arrived in the fortnightly letters from my grandmother. Over time, these photographs took on a strange pink hue caused by the instability of the colour dyes used in their printing. These images spoke to me not about a past that was rapidly disappearing, but about the uncertainties that characterised the present.

One image in particular exerts a powerful effect. It shows three people seated at a narrow table. At the left-hand edge of the picture is a man who looks to be in his early thirties. He has shoulder-length dark hair that is receding at the temples, and is wearing thick black-rimmed glasses and a short-sleeved white shirt unbuttoned at the neck. He is not a handsome man. His lack of obvious good looks is accentuated by the attractiveness of the much younger woman seated next to him—my cousin—and around whose shoulders he has draped his left arm. 'Koukla!' (Doll) my grandmother would exclaim each time she showed me other photographs of the young woman whose light-brown eyes are matched by the colour of her hair. This pronouncement usually marked the commencement of one of my grandmother's favourite topics of discussion: the unfortunate choices made by the members of her family. This preoccupation stemmed from her impossibly high estimation of the attractiveness of her children and grandchildren. But it also spoke to the reality that, in the arrangement of her own unhappy marriage, she had had no choice.

That the young woman and the man are celebrating their betrothal is testified by a table laden with presents that appears in the background of the photograph, as well as by the actions of the third figure: a boy of no more than six or seven—the young woman's brother, also my cousin—who has raised himself a few inches off his chair, turned his body towards the couple and, in a gesture borrowed from the adult world, holds his glass aloft in celebration.

Brought up in an environment where appearances matter, I remember being aware of the disparity between the couple in the photograph. But the primary focus of my attention was the young boy. This stemmed partly from feelings of rivalry: Was he taller or shorter than me? Would you say that his clothes were better or uglier that mine? That I was roughly the same age as him contributed to the intensity of these feelings—as did my mother's unwavering commitment to the world of which he was part. But as powerful as these feelings were, I realise now that they were the outcrop of something more complicated. This was the sense that the boy, whose gesture of celebration both impressed and infuriated me, was living my life in place of me. Not the life I was leading in our home in the suburbs of Newcastle. But the life that we had left behind.

II

In an essay on their own family's history of emigration, the writer Masha Gessen calls this the sensation of a parallel life. They link this sensation to the moment when a life proceeding according to the dictates of tradition and history changes course. In themselves, these parallel lives are no better or worse than the lives forged elsewhere. The difference has to do, first, with the realisation that they are destined to remain just possibilities and, second, with the way in which they are endowed with all the unresolved emotions that accompany the break. The parallel life is lived elsewhere. But it also shadows our everyday actions. Gessen recalls watching their parents preparing the documents required for an exit visa to leave the Soviet Union. 'For thirty-nine years, ever since my parents took those documents to the visa office, I have felt so precarious that I lay no claim to someone I "really am." That someone is a sequence of choices, and the question is: Will my next choice be conscious, and will my ability to make it be unfettered?'

Gessen describes this sensation from the point of view of an adult self, negotiating an identity in a world full of choices and possibilities. Thinking about my own history, I'm inclined to believe that the sensation of a parallel life is no less powerful for children growing up in a world determined by the choices of their parents. My evidence for this is the strange hold exercised on me by the photograph of the young boy. Looking at the confidence of his gesture, his ability to place himself at the centre of the celebration, I knew with some certainty that the world in which I moved was nothing more than a hastily arranged configuration, liable to fall apart at any moment, and that my proper life was happening elsewhere, without me.

III

The photographs in my mother's album helped me to understand what it meant to inhabit this other life: its ways of dressing, celebrating milestones and being with others. In these matters, the two worlds seemed to exist side by side. But what the photographs also showed me was something unique to the world revealed in these images: a sense of what it looks like to be comfortable in one's own skin. And because the people in the photographs seemed to know me better than I knew them, they also held open the promise that I might find a way to return to this other life and reclaim a history that was rightfully mine.

How do we deal with the legacies of these other lives? Of moments of choice that leave us suspended? Karim Aïnouz's *Mariner of the Mountains* (2021) documents the filmmaker's journey to his father's place of birth in Kabylia, in northern Algeria. Growing up in Brazil, he only knew his father from stories told by his mother, Iracema, and from photographs taken when his parents were foreign students studying in the United States. The first meeting between father and son occurred when the filmmaker was eighteen, in a cafe in Paris, where his father was living with his wife and daughter. 'I grew up imagining Majid as a cross between Yuri Gagarin and Che Guevara,' he recalls. 'He was neither. He was an ordinary man ... He didn't look like a member of a secret clan, who grew up in the mountains and survived many wars. So many years wanting to ask so many questions. Suddenly, we didn't have much to say to one another.'

Long after this meeting and in the wake of Iracema's death, he decides to travel to Algeria. His motivations for doing so are not entirely clear. The trip is a chance to see the village where his father was born. But at a deeper level it is an opportunity to understand the forces that determined the course of the relationship between his parents. The details of this relationship are lightly sketched: their initial encounter at a social event for foreign students in Washington; Majid's departure for Colorado; Iracema's return to Wisconsin to complete her research on the DNA of red seaweed; the intense exchange of letters that followed; her relocation to Colorado. The backdrop to these events is the political turmoil in their respective homelands: the military coup in Brazil and the war of independence in Algeria. In 1963 Aïnouz's pregnant mother returned to Brazil, while his father travelled back to Algeria. Saying goodbye, he promised that, soon, they would reunite and start a life together in Algeria.

That this promise was never kept is the starting point for the filmmaker's attempt to imagine another life. And not to simply imagine this life: to trace its presence in the images that document his parents' past and his own journey to Kabylia. Like the photographs of Majid and Iracema during their time in the United States, the images of the Algerian men going about their business, socialising or just passing the time staring at the ocean suggest the possibility of encountering one's self at another time and at another place. Drawn along by the filmmaker's melancholic voiceover, the images allow us to glean the outlines of this unlived life.

Arriving at his father's home village high in the mountains, the filmmaker encounters a small boy on his way to school. As the boy gazes at the camera, Aïnouz speculates on what his history would have been like if his life had followed the same path: 'Would I have moved to Algiers and become an engineer? Would I have found a wife and had twin kids to raise and dreamt of living in Zurich? Or maybe I'd never have left this village until I reached 54, when I'd have travelled to Fortaleza to see where Iracema was born? I'd be now staring at the Atlantic wondering how my life would have been ... It would have been my life inside out.' A little later, he is introduced to a man who shares the same name and year of birth, a businessman. Sitting in his car, the man insists on showing the filmmaker his identity card. Beside him are his two children: a small girl, who remains unfazed by the camera's attention, and a young boy, who hides his face, as if to guard himself from the consequences of some damaging revelation.

Slowly, the hospitality of the villagers with whom he bears various forms of familial connection leads him to construct a figure he calls 'Karim Aïnouz upside-down', a man born in the same village as his father, who continues to live in the mountains, makes a living as a nightlife impresario, yet also finds the time to tend grapevines and make his own wine. He ponders what it would be like to step into the shoes of this other Karim Aïnouz. 'I never thought about it before, but suddenly I started thinking that maybe I could live here, restore some of those old houses and grow a bunch of grapevines, make wine and open a nightclub.' The denouement occurs when he visits the village cemetery and notices that most of the headstones bear the same name: Aïnouz. 'Suddenly it all started to tremble, as if I were on the edge of a cliff. I felt hollow ... I was afraid I'd fall into a grave and never come out again.' The feeling of vertigo causes him to flee. Standing at the stern of the boat as it slowly pulls away from the harbour in Algiers, he wonders if all that he experienced in Kabylia was real or just a dream. Or if Karim Aïnouz is leaving or being left behind.

Mariner of the Mountains, dir. Karim Aïnouz, 2021

IV

By the time my parents had earned enough money to pay for a holiday back to Cyprus, thirteen years had passed since our departure. During this time, they went from being in the prime of their lives to being middle-aged, physically and mentally worn down by the routines of shop life. The trip back occurred near the end of my final year in high school. The beauty of the island and the warmth of the people created a feeling of homecoming that, in the years that followed, was never able to be replicated. This had to do with the time when we were there—just prior to the uncertainties that lay beyond the horizon of high school. Each subsequent trip brought to the surface some aspect of the person I was becoming that was too hard to reconcile with life on the island. Deciding on the type of degree to study for, finding a job, moving in and out of relationships, determining when and with whom to start a family. These things can happen quickly. But they can also take years to play out. Over time, the feeling of precariousness that characterised the years following our arrival in Australia was replaced by a set of demands that fixed my attention firmly on the here and now.

For my mother, the here and now remains always elsewhere. This is how she acknowledges the consequences of having made a choice and finds the means to hold on to what this choice takes away. In her mind, Cyprus remains free from the contingencies that are part of our life in Australia, a place where the actions and behaviour of people are part of a continuum. Each spring, she returns to the house that was bequeathed to her as the eldest daughter. She enjoys the long months of summer with her siblings, cousins and in-laws. When the weather starts turning cooler in late October, she prepares to return to Sydney. Picking her up from the airport, her bags laden with walnuts, bottles of zivania and packets of loukomia, her response to our questions is always the same: 'They're all fine. They send their love and look forward to seeing you next summer.'

My own sense of how the people there have changed was formed over the course of a number of visits—originally with my parents and, later, with my own wife and daughter. During these visits I came to know the young boy in the faded colour photograph, not well, but in the familiar manner that binds cousins. I came to know some of the ups and downs that characterised his life and the lives of other members of my extended family. I also came to realise that my curiosity about their lives would never be matched by their curiosity about my life in Australia.

Unlike many of my other cousins, except for a brief unhappy period studying in Greece and occasional vacations abroad, the boy in the photograph had never left Cyprus. The town where he lived was the town where generations of our family had been born and raised. One way or another, he knew just about everybody in the town. And they knew him: a good-looking, educated young man from a respected family. It was only a matter of time, people thought, before he settled down and married a woman worthy of his good looks and upbringing.

During our conversations, he would make fun of his preference for the comforts of Cypriot life over what he believed to be the harshness of life in other countries. 'I'm happy to stay where I am,' he would say. *'Why would I want to leave?'* Indeed, there was little obvious reason for him to leave the island. Its high standard of living had been achieved off the back of a booming tourism and services-based economy—primarily, banking and finance services. Vastly different in experiences and opportunities, the generation that my cousin belongs to inherited from previous generations an entrepreneurial flair that comes from being citizens of a small island. In my cousin's case, his good looks, fluency in English and easy charm led to a career in real estate, facilitating property deals for foreign nationals.

During my visits we would occasionally meet at night for a drink near the harbour and he would tell me about his day spent escorting clients from place to place. Because of the range of people with whom he came into contact, his view of life was broad, yet it was also narrow in the range of what he saw of the lives of these people. During these evening meetings, he would sometimes ask me questions about my life—if it involved the same level of stress, if I was able to make enough money doing what I did and how it was that I ended up teaching in a university.

Over the course of a number of these conversations, I came to know more about the reasons why he had chosen to remain on the island. In his early twenties, he fell in love with a young woman from the United Kingdom who was in Cyprus on a working holiday. That he could be with a woman and not have to immediately commit to marriage was something he found liberating. Not long into their relationship, the young woman fell pregnant and, for a few years after the birth of their daughter, they lived together as a family. The decision to remain unmarried did cause problems with his family. But most of the time he was happy to put up with their warnings about the consequences of his decision. The real problems came later, and were to do with the differences in expectations between himself and his partner—small things, really, to do with his daughter's upbringing. Was it right for his partner to continue to work and focus on her career? How often did they need to make themselves available to his family and relatives? How much responsibility should he take in the daily care of his daughter? Mixed in with these issues was his partner's feelings of homesickness and her desire to raise her daughter nearer to her own family.

No doubt other things played a part. After the separation, he feared that his partner would leave the island and he would not be able to see his daughter. To make matters worse, he had to deal with the recriminations of those members of his family who saw his troubles as confirmation of everything they had predicted. It was around this time that he came to see his relationship to his family differently. They still kept in regular contact. Their health and well-being were still a primary concern. But now he felt that their lives could no longer serve as a model for his own. Their experiences and choices were fundamentally different.

The last time we spoke, his life had settled down. His former partner was living a short distance away. She had met someone else and, for the time being, was content to call the island home. Now, his life is dominated by the routines of being a single parent: negotiating pick-ups and drop-offs, ensuring that childcare is in place and doing what he can to be a good father. Compared to the problems experienced by other couples who have gone through similar break-ups, he said, he feels lucky.

When he told me about these events, I thought of how much time had passed since the moment captured in the photograph in my mother's album. The difference between the person whom I got to know—his humour, generosity and candour—and the type of person I had associated with his image was a matter not just of age and time, but also of attitude and fate. It was the difference between someone whose imagined life is a series of scenes held together by feelings of rivalry and second-hand stories, and someone whose life is marked by the pitfalls and pleasures that are part of living. Despite the differences in our histories, our lives came together in a way that has made a friendship possible. This friendship has allowed me to see my own history differently. Now, when I think about this other life, it, too, is marked by choices made and decisions lived with.

V

In Gessen's reflections on their life both before and after emigration, two moments stand out as defining. The first took place in the months just prior to their family's emigration to the United States. Gessen remembers the overwhelming feeling of belonging experienced while listening to the singing of a group of Jewish cultural activists meeting in secret in the woods outside Moscow. 'I was surrounded by strangers, sitting, as we were, on logs laid across the grass, and I remember their faces to this day. I looked at them and thought, *This is who I am.*' The second moment occurred a couple of years after their arrival in the United States. Leaning against a wall at a gay dance at Yale, they remember the exhilaration of looking around and thinking, '*This is who I could be.*' 'What the syncope of emigration had meant for me,' they conclude, 'was the difference between discovering who I was—the experience I had in the woods outside of Moscow—and discovering who I could be—the experience I had at that dance. It was a moment of choice and, thanks to the "break in my destiny," I was aware of it.'

For my cousin, who had never felt the need to leave his home, there had also been a moment of choice that, once made, transformed everything that came before and followed after. This moment is different from the one faced by my parents when they made the decision to leave their homes and families. But in both cases, we are dealing with a moment when something other is imagined, a moment precarious *and* exciting, when a life goes from something familiar and bound by clear expectations, to something that one has to fashion largely on one's own. Moreover, in both cases, there is the matter of how to make peace with the afterlife of these choices.

This is why, in the midst of his good humour and conviviality, something in my cousin's manner—a way of pausing to acknowledge his own weaknesses and failings, an awareness of the fragility of his relationships—tells me that he, too, has experienced the sensation of a parallel life. Perhaps if I were to show him the faded photograph of himself in my mother's album he would look at the young boy, and, like me, be impressed by the confidence of his gesture. Recognising himself in this figure, he might also come to believe that, despite everything that has happened, despite the distance that he has travelled and the decisions made, he might use this strangely coloured photograph to reconcile himself to the call of this other life. The life that had continued without him.

4
The Keys to the House

I

The Girl from the Sea, dir. John Conomos, 2018

'They gave me your things in a brown paper bag. I asked to see you, to be convinced that what they were telling me was true.' What 'they'—the doctors and nurses—were telling the narrator in Antigone Kefala's novella 'Conversations with Mother' is summed up in three short words: 'You had died.' Perhaps it's because she had assumed the worst had passed and things were looking up for her ailing mother that the narrator finds this so hard to believe and why she needs to see the body, for herself: 'And there you were behind the glass, on this trolley, in white, with your white hair, I scaled the steps and went behind the glass to see you, touch you, stroke your forehead, your hair.' The situation of a narrator addressing an absent loved one is far from unusual. In Kefala's rendition of this familiar trope, grief crosses paths with indignation and disbelief. 'I have written to everyone about your death,' she tells her mother, 'so that all of us can be up in arms about it.' It's one thing to accept the death of a loved one, the narrator's indignation suggests. It's another thing entirely to accept her disappearance. 'I was telling Elizabeth over lunch: "No, no, I shall never accept this disappearance, whatever they say ... everyone says ... however inevitable ... no ..."'

'What a disappearance! What a total disappearance! What an impossible disappearance!' The challenge that drives the narrator's reflections can be put simply: how to render the impact of this disappearance on a world that has been lessened, stripped of an essential dimension, at the same time as it has become strangely enlivened by the shockwaves generated by this terrible event. 'Saturday night in Paramatta Road, the darkness of the night, the lights in the park, the terrible idea that you had disappeared for ever took my breath away, a terrible knowledge that had gathered for a second in the feeble lights across the street, the empty blackness of the night.' The recollections, observations and outbursts that document the narrator's response to this terrible knowledge ensure that her mother remains present as something other than a memory, as something whose afterlife is imprinted on the rhythms and textures of everyday existence.

II

'When a person dies,' writes John Berger, 'they leave behind, for those who knew them, an emptiness, a space: the space has contours and is different for each person mourned. This space with its contours is the person's *likeness* and is what the artist searches for when making a living portrait.' How are the terms and conditions of this likeness reconfigured when the portrait is filmic rather than literary? What elements give the filmic portrait its distinctive engagement with the disappeared? Early in John Conomos's video *The Girl from the Sea* (2018) we observe the director sitting at a large dining table scrutinising a selection of black-and-white photographs of his late mother, Maria. The photographs illustrate some of the biographical details described in his voiceover narration: her arrival in Australia from Kythera as a girl of eleven or twelve, accompanied by her two sisters; her time spent living with her aunts in the northern New South Wales towns of Warialda and Inverell; her marriage to George, the director's father, and their life together running a milk bar in the Sydney suburb of Tempe; her devastation at George's sudden early death and her subsequent marriage to Zacharias. The director also recounts the illnesses that plagued his mother's later years and his attempts to break through her 'encroaching Alzheimer's muteness'.

These details furnish the outlines of a life that resembled so many other lives that were part of the waves of human migration that took place in the years leading up to and immediately following the Second World War. But it is not the generalities of his mother's life that Conomos endeavours to convey. Rather, it is her personhood and how this was expressed in an all-encompassing labour of homemaking—as a vocation, a duty, an act of love. To have been the beneficiary of this is the filmmaker's privilege. To find the creative language to commemorate its passing is his obligation. The purpose of the photographs is to drive a work of remembrance in which the presence of the magnifying glass in the director's hand acts as a proxy for the camera's investigations of these images. The slow zooms in to the photographs that spotlight a certain detail or facial expression, the panning movements across the surface of the black-and-white prints that bring images of the past into an engagement with the present, the dissolves that establish a relationship between two or more images: this is how the camera functions as an extension of the director's gaze and approaches the residues of his mother's life through its own distinctive ways of seeing.

The Girl from the Sea, dir. John Conomos, 2018

In the opening moments the camera guides the viewer through the front garden of the family home in the Sydney suburb of Hurstville. Once inside the house, it peers into the almost-empty front bedroom. The dark wooden bed frame and mattress, stripped of sheets and blankets, are the vestiges of a life that, little by little, is losing its grip on this place. And for the next fifteen minutes or so, the camera will move in and out of these rooms, surveying the remaining pieces of furniture and the gently billowing curtains and venetian blinds. Its scrutiny of these almost-empty rooms works in concert with the director's voiceover to conjure a labour that made them greater than the sum of their parts.

When the camera sweeps into the kitchen it considers a collection of keys spread across the benchtop. Their sheer number poses a challenge to the mind. What do these keys open? To what tasks do they belong? Elevated above their station by the camera's close-up observation, they remind us of cinema's capacity to reveal elements of everyday life that are usually overlooked or excluded and, at the same time, to bring about a productive estrangement. Guided by the camera's way of seeing, we approach the world not from above, as

The Girl from the Sea, dir. John Conomos, 2018

the film theorist Siegfried Kracauer so memorably observes, but from 'under the table'.

Now, if this is true of the camera's rendition of the world in general, it is doubly so in the case of those films that take stock of a home space. In Robert Frank's Home Improvements (1985), for example, the video camera operates as an extension of the filmmaker's roving eye as it moves through the world. The handheld shots of the artworks scattered around his studio; the footage of his partner, the artist June Leaf, inside their car watching the waves battering the foreshore near their home in Nova Scotia; the close-up shots of a fly moving along a windowpane: these sights and sounds evoke a fragile sense of happiness and provide the backdrop to Frank's ruminations about those closest to him. After visiting his son in a psychiatric treatment centre, he uses the video camera to record his troubled thoughts during the journey home: 'As I walk back from the visit with Pablo ... I always have hope, but I realize that ... I would try. And I think it means a lot to him if I try. He knows when I try. I just don't know how long I can do it.' The jumpy footage of the nondescript hospital buildings and the moments when the filmmaker pauses to gather his thoughts ground the images in his physical and emotional state of being. They encapsulate a way of employing the video camera that the film scholar Philippe Dubois describes as 'a form of looking and thinking that functions continuously and as if live with regard to everything'. The video camera as always present, always within easy reach of hand, eye and voice.

In Chantal Akerman's *No Home Movie* (2015) the video camera also functions as an extension of the filmmaker's eye as she moves through the rooms of her elderly mother's apartment in Brussels. But at other times it remains resolutely fixed in place, observing and listening in on the conversations between the director and her mother at the kitchen table, or taking up a spot in the lounge room or hallway and patiently watching the apartment's occupants. During one such sequence the camera is positioned outside the partially opened door to a room bathed in light from a window in the background. Through the doorway we can see the silhouette of the filmmaker's mother, Natalia, and, once or twice, the filmmaker herself. The camera's focus is on the person *and* the space around the person—its structures, impediments, the quality of light. This dual focus locates Akerman's portrait of her mother between the two poles that have long been regarded as intrinsic to the form of viewing enabled by a camera: on the one hand, an acute feeling of proximity to the events and individuals portrayed on screen and, on the other, the impression of an unbridgeable distance, in time as much as in space. 'We are beholding a world which has gone beneath the waves,' Virginia Woolf observes about the people and events in early newsreels. 'Brides are emerging from the Abbey; ushers are ardent; mothers are tearful; guests are joyful; and it is all over and done with.' In *No Home Movie* the camera's attentiveness to the material qualities of the apartment conveys a sense of home as determined by the emotional closeness that binds mother and daughter, and as always already lost.

III

The Girl from the Sea, John Conomos, 2018

In *The Girl from the Sea* the camera's graceful, almost rhythmic slow-motion pans provide an inventory of what remains of Maria's life and convey a powerful choreographic presence, aided by the inclusion on the soundtrack of the rise and fall of waves lapping the shore of an unseen beach. This audio element reminds us of Maria's ancestral home on the island of Kythera. It also affirms that in the video Conomos is constructing home both as an actual place made from bricks and mortar, and as an image, formed by the interaction of material elements and the imagination. This interplay is amplified by the superimposition onto the gently billowing curtains of some of the photographs that were laid out on the dining room table and the inclusion of brief excerpts from films that stand in for the director's recollection of events that he either experienced directly or heard about second-hand. The first involves a story told by his mother's cousin about Maria as a small child, scrambling down the mountainside near her home village of Karavas. In the director's mind, this story recalls Ingrid Bergman's flight up the volcano in Roberto Rossellini's *Stromboli* (1950). The second involves the day when the filmmaker witnessed his mother's response to the phone call telling her of George's death. The impact of this event is conveyed by the inclusion of the moment near the finale of Orson Welles's *The Lady from Shanghai* (1947) when the staggering protagonist slides into the mouth of an amusement-park mechanical monster.

Based on the connections between different images, and between images and the memories they inspire, this method of appropriating images uses the cinema to evoke a threshold—between documentary and fiction, past and present, memory and forgetting. 'The idea is to create connections,' Jean-Luc Godard explains. 'Just as stars are drawn closer to one another, even as they move further away from one another, held together by physical laws, to form a constellation, certain thoughts are drawn closer together and form one or several images.' In Conomos's work the connections formed speak to a gap in one's knowledge that is a consequence of the displacements caused by migration. Near the start of the multi-screen video installation *Album Leaves* (1999), for instance, Conomos wanders through a graveyard looking for his father's resting place—mumbling to himself as he moves along the rows. When he comes to the plot where George is buried, his words suggest both relief and disappointment: 'This is it here ... It's not what I imagined it to be.' His words trail off, to be picked up at a later point. Looking down at the grave, he muses: 'It's so hard to capture him ... You never do, do you? You just chase your own shadows.' These simple yet evocative words allude to everything that gets lost in the passage from one generation to the next, from one culture to the next. The restless, never-finished engagement with images that defines Conomos's method is, on one level at least, an attempt to compensate for this loss—a method of constructing knowledge in the face of its possible extinguishment.

IV

The other way to describe this endeavour is as an activity of homemaking. In an account of some of the changes that characterise modernity, Berger contrasts an archaic notion of home, understood as a fixed centre that enables its inhabitants to maintain a sense of continuity between the past and the present, the living and the dead, with a more contemporary notion of home as built from scratch. The instigator for this change is the large-scale migrations of people from village to city and from country to country over the past two centuries. For those whose lives were reshaped by these migrations, the traditional notion of home as something predetermined is replaced by a structure built on the accretion of habit, repetition and, above all, memory. 'The mortar which holds the improvised "home" together—even for a child—is memory. Within it, visible, tangible mementoes are arranged—photos, trophies, souvenirs—but the roof and four walls which safeguard the lives within, these are invisible, intangible, and biographical.'

In *The Girl from the Sea*, Conomos's agenda is twofold: to recount the extraordinary spirit that marked his mother's life and to safeguard the memories on which the home-space is founded. He tells us of his mother's optimism, effervescence and will to live. He recalls her urging him to be less lazy and more appreciative of life's possibilities. He alludes to the scandal she caused by announcing her intention to marry Zacharias—too soon after George's death, in the eyes of friends and family—as well as the fatalism and pathos conveyed by her singing the Doris Day classic 'Que Sera, Sera'. Perhaps most poignantly of all he recounts her enthusiasm for collecting miniature porcelain figurines. His account of her passion for arranging these delicately wrought objects into scenes of an idealised domestic life is a foretelling of Conomos's own endeavours with images and sounds. The work of homemaking in which the filmmaker is engaged is not only about continuity between past and present. It is also about the future—how we recall the person that we will become.

V

The concluding section of *The Girl from the Sea* begins with a shot of the filmmaker standing in front of a microphone and reading from a script. Up to this point, his presence has registered as a body hunched over the photographs spread across the dining table or as a voiceover recounting the details of his mother's life. Now we see him as someone who has reached a point in his life when the ailments and afflictions that marked his mother's later years weigh heavily on him. The issue, then, is age, not simply as the sum of so many years of existence, but also as a form of mutuality that binds our existence to those who came before. In *The Girl from the Sea* this mutuality is both a burden and a comfort. It establishes continuity between the generations and anticipates the travails that lie ahead.

In the concluding narration, the filmmaker describes how, during the final years of his mother's life, when renal failure and the gradual worsening of her Alzheimer's disease made communication more and more difficult, he would take her to the seaside, and the two of them would pass the time watching colourful boats bobbing up and down. 'What ensued between us then,' he recalls, 'was a kind of deeply felt monosyllabic form of Rogerian psychotherapy, a longing, an attempt to reanimate your being, your shared existence with mine.'

'When a being is no more, the world narrows all of a sudden, and a part of reality collapses,' writes the philosopher Vinciane Despret. 'Each time an existence disappears, it is a piece of the universe of sensations that fades away.' But there are also moments of continuation. 'Everything I see, I hear, I remember, I touch, leads back to you,' writes Kefala in 'Conversations with Mother'. 'It does not matter how remote, how unconnected, how far, everything leads back.' In the novella, the narrator projects her grief onto a world that has changed fundamentally, yet whose sensations retain the imprint of her mother's presence. This world must be held accountable for her mother's disappearance. The trips to the movies or the theatre, the visits by friends who offer support and bring with them their own troubles, the sudden change in the weather and its effect on the flowers in the garden: these events provide the backdrop for ongoing conversations between mother and daughter. In the context of the narrator's grief, they also suggest a world too ready to resume its flow.

The end of the novella does not bring acceptance or an easing of this grief. Instead, the shift in tone stems from an image in which the indicators of time's passing carry with them a suggestion of survival. Walking through Sydney's Botanical Gardens, the narrator describes the trees as marked by a 'human heaviness': 'The Moreton Bay figs with those heavy shapes made of granite, and the olive trees, full of little breasts coming out everywhere, as if a series of humans that have disappeared to leave only some vital part of their bodies transfixed into bark, to survive longer.'

The Girl from the Sea, dir. John Conomos, 2018

In the concluding section of *The Girl from the Sea* the filmmaker's engagements with the world also offer an image that recasts the feelings of loss associated with his mother's death. Introduced during his account of the trips to the seashore with his mother, it is of two sailing boats moving in opposite directions across an expanse of ocean. This image illustrates the filmmaker's account of the trips to the seashore and provides something that exceeds the capacities of the narration: a direct engagement with the world, its colour, energy and movement. The azure water and matching sky, the bright white billowing sails of the boats, their slow-motion movement up and down and across the water: these elements distance us from the almost-empty rooms of the soon-to-be abandoned house. They mark the point at which the labour of homemaking—of creating a place where one might shelter from the sudden turns of fate, embodied by George's death—coincides with a drive to venture forth and place oneself in the path of these blows. This is a conception of homemaking in which the accretion of habit, repetition and memory work hand in hand with a responsiveness to the possibilities and as yet undetermined qualities of the present. The image of the two sailing boats making their way across the horizon is, finally, a way to commemorate Maria's passing and to capture what the filmmaker in his concluding words describes as her unique gift, the 'gift of being vital to life itself'.[2]

---

2   *The Girl from the Sea* was acquired by the Art Gallery of NSW in 2019. It can be viewed at vimeo.com/513204049

5
The Phantom's Call

I

Estrella (Icíar Bollaín). In Víctor Erice, *El Sur*, dir. Víctor Erice, 1983

'Never, not even at that solemn moment,' the Spanish director Víctor Erice recalls, 'did we imagine that, with the passage of time, the cinema was going to be an essential element of our memory, the recipient capable of containing the images that best reflect human experience at the end of the [twentieth] century.' He links this attachment to the legacy of specific events. 'I am talking about people from my generation, those born in the destruction, and the times of silence, after our Civil War. Real and symbolic orphans, cinema adopted us, offering us an extraordinary consolation, the feeling of belonging to the world.' In Erice's films, this consolation and feeling of belonging is tied to cinema's ability to conjure a past that remains unfinished. In his 1983 film *El Sur* (The South), for example, this unfinished business is associated with the female narrator's father, Agustín (Omero Antonutti), and the circumstances surrounding his decision to leave his home in the south of Spain. The emblem for this mystery is the image, reproduced in a number of reviews and publications on the director's work, of the film's narrator, Estrella (played as a fifteen-year-old by Icíar Bollaín), holding Agustín's silver pendulum up to the wintry morning light filtering through her bedroom window. 'That day at sunrise,' her adult self recalls in the voiceover that accompanies this moment, 'when I found his pendulum under my pillow, I felt that everything had changed, that he would never come home.'

The events of this fateful morning trigger Estrella's recollections of her family's arrival in an unnamed city in the North, their life in the two-storey house located on its outskirts and the lead-up to her First Communion, when her family played host to two visitors from the South: her father's mother, Rosario (Germaine Montero), and Milagros (Rafaela Aparicio), the woman who had primary responsibility for his upbringing. Their arrival provides Estrella with an opportunity to find out what drove Agustín to leave his home in the South. But it's clear from Milagros's equivocal responses to Estrella's questions about her father's difficult relationship with his Francoist father that the film's interest is not to uncover the reasons behind his decision. Rather, it is to render the impact that this mystery had on her childhood—its haunting by a place that demands something of her.

II

In 'Notes on the Phantom', the psychoanalyst Nicolas Abraham claims that while all the departed may return to ensnare the living, it is those individuals who took secrets to the grave who are destined to haunt. The role of the phantom is to objectify the gap created in the subject's psyche by this concealment. 'It works like a ventriloquist,' Abraham explains, 'like a stranger within the subject's own mental topography.' In *El Sur*, Estrella's recollections of the effect of Agustín's past on her childhood centre on her encounters with a series of phantoms. There are the phantoms that look back at her from the strangely coloured picture postcards she keeps in a cigar box and which she relies on to construct her own sense of the South. Even more significant is the phantom whose name is first encountered on an envelope in Agustín's study: Irene Ríos. Shortly after this discovery, Estrella comes across her father's motorbike parked in front of the town's cinema. Perusing one of the posters outside the building, she learns that the name written over and over again on her father's envelope belongs to the film's co-star.

Erice then does something that occurs elsewhere in the film. With a pronounced upward tilt of the camera, the film leaves behind the viewpoint of its central character, standing outside the cinema. In the scene that follows we witness an encounter that belongs as much to the film's own operations as it does to Estrella's recollections: we see Agustín seated in the darkened theatre looking up at the screen on which Irene Ríos (played by Aurore Clément) is performing in a black-and-white melodrama, *Flor en la sombra* (Flower in the Shadow). As Irene sits in front of a dressing-room mirror brushing her hair, she appears to look back at Agustín. Their reunion lasts only a few moments. But this is long enough to clarify a key aspect of the film's rendition of Estrella's recollections: their occupation of a space that is neither wholly inside nor wholly outside the consciousness of the central character, a space in which remembrance is taken over by the power of images to not only speak for our history, but also to spirit it away.

III

'The ways in which we do not know things are just as important (and perhaps even more important) as the ways in which know them,' writes the philosopher Giorgio Agamben. Not-knowing should not be seen as a lack, he asserts. Rather, it informs everything we do. In Erice's films, this recognition is tied to an experience of images. His first film, *El espíritu de la colmena* (The Spirit of the Beehive, 1973), begins with a van approaching a small village on the Castilian plain. The date, we are told in a subtitle, is around 1940. The excitement of the children is because the van carries the reels of film and projection equipment that will transform the village's rundown town hall into a cinema. The film to be screened later that evening is James Whale's 1931 version of *Frankenstein*. A woman who serves as the village crier announces the cost of admission: one peseta for adults and two reales for children. In Erice's films, details that in another context might be considered incidental play an important role in establishing a precise sense of place. In the scene that follows, we watch the village children arranging their chairs in front of the screen. At the door, the impresario responsible for bringing the film to the village is collecting the pesetas and reales. 'I hope it's good this time,' a woman tells him. 'It's magnificent,' he replies. 'Don't start a fire, now,' he warns another woman, who has brought along a brazier to keep herself warm. Quickly, the barn-like room is filled with villagers excitedly chatting among themselves.

When the lights dim and the projector starts rolling, a man dressed in a tuxedo appears on screen. Cloaked in the guise of a content warning, his remarks prime the audience for the story to come, a story about 'the great mysteries of creation: life and death'. After he walks off stage, the screen fades to black. When it fades back up, it takes a few seconds for us to realise that what we are watching is not the start of *Frankenstein*, but an unnamed figure tending an apiary. That the man's protective attire and awkward movements conjure images of the monster in Whale's film is one way in which Erice encourages us to view the emotions conjured inside the cinema as continuous with life outside—a life that is marked by an acute sense of loss and grief.

'Though nothing can bring back the happy moments we spent together, I pray that God grant me the joy of seeing you again. That's been my constant prayer ever since we parted during the war.' Conveyed as a voiceover, these words link the scene of the man tending the bees, who we will come to know as Fernando (Fernando Fernán Gómez), to the scene that follows of an as yet unnamed woman (Teresa Gimpera) sitting at her desk, writing to an absent lover.

The manner in which the woman's words play over the top of a close-up of Fernando's half-hidden face prompts us to question their provenance as well as their intended receiver. Voices bleeding across scenes, footsteps announcing the presence of creatures that are as much imagined as real, train whistles reaching out to us through the night air: this is how Erice uses the properties of sound to evoke a domain of experience that cuts across boundaries. Thus, when Fernando finishes his work with the bees and makes his way home, past the hall where the villagers are watching the screening of Whale's film, Erice floods the street with the whirring sound of the projector's mechanisms and snatches of the movie's dialogue. A few moments later, these sounds penetrate the thick walls and windows of Fernando's study, prompting him to put down the magazine he had started reading. When he opens the large honeycomb windows onto a small balcony, the slow forward track of the camera that follows behind seems to be driven by a need to trace the source of a sound whose volume and acoustic range expand and contract in a manner that enables it to connect otherwise discrete zones of activity.

Even at this early point, it is possible to glean at least two aspects of cinematic experience that are central to the stories told in Erice's films: on the one hand, cinema as an actual place—noisy, squeezed together, intrusive—and, on the other, cinema as a way of relating to images and sounds that are defined by their capacity to escape their moorings. In *El espíritu de la colmena* this capacity is realised in an image that brings together the two sides of the film's operations: as a one-time-only event recorded by the camera and as the telling of a fictional story. It occurs when the camera, enticed by the sounds penetrating Fernando's study, returns to the hall where the villagers are watching the film. From the mass of faces gathered in front of the screen, it picks out the two young girls who serve as the film's central characters, Isabel (Isabel Tellería) and Ana (Ana Torrent). After a few moments, it becomes clear that it is Ana, the younger of the two, whose responses hold a special interest. Cutting between the scene from Whale's film that shows the first meeting of the monster and the little village girl who befriends him, and a hand-held shot of Ana gazing intently up at the screen, the film captures that 'unrepeatable moment' when the stunned responses of the young actress watching the movie for the first time become indistinguishable from the reactions of the character that she plays.

'I sincerely believe that it's the best moment I've ever captured on film,' the director confessed to an interviewer. 'It was an actual screening. She was really seeing the movie. He [Luis Cuadrado, the film's cinematographer] captured her reaction to the encounter between the monster and the little girl. So it was an unrepeatable moment, one that could never be "directed".' In the same interview, he observed that, in a film made in 'a very premeditated style', the key moment had escaped premeditation: 'I think that's the crack through which the aspect of film that records reality bursts through into every kind of fictional narrative ... But without the substratum of fiction, it too would fail to acquire its fullest sense as an image recording reality.'

For Erice, the affective force of Ana's reaction comes from a dual action, whereby the fiction created by the director is taken over by a response that both serves and supersedes its guiding structures. In *El espíritu de la colmena* two factors give this moment its particular quality. First, its grounding in a child's view of the world. In a written tribute to Charlie Chaplin's *City Lights* (1931), Erice claims that, at its most memorable, the experience of cinema creates an impression of 'passing over a threshold, as if images revealed life's multiple truths. Moments difficult to describe, belonging to those primordial stories we hold in our memories, in which often the silhouette of the child and of the adolescent we once were are present.' The second factor is Erice's insistence on embedding this 'unrepeatable moment' in the mass of bodies pressed together in the crowded hall. Indeed, our response to Ana's reaction has a lot to do with the presence of the young girl seated immediately to her right, who covers her eyes when the monster appears from behind the bushes. Seen for just these brief moments, the unidentified young girl reminds us of those forces, personalities and histories that make up the life of the village, a life that both precedes the film and continues after its cessation.

Ana (Ana Torrent). In *El espíritu de la comena* (The Spirit of the Beehive), dir. Víctor Erice, 1973

Everything that happens to Ana during the course of *El espíritu de la colmena*—her attempts to clarify the nature of the monster (*real or fake? spirit or phantom?*), her relationship with the wounded rebel soldier, her flight from her father and encounter with the monster on the riverbank—is designed to shed light on the capacity of this moment to subsist within the social realities of Spain in the dark years immediately after the end of the Civil War. The return to a child's view of the world is not an escape from the pressures and restrictions of the social world. Rather, it is how the film tests the limits of these pressures and restrictions, and solicits forms of engagement that they actively repress. The unrepeatable moment embodied in Ana's response is also a moment of renewal—for both the cinema and the social world in which it occurs.

IV

This detour to a film made ten years prior to *El Sur* helps to clarify the implications generated by the decision to leave the eight-year-old Estrella's perspective outside the cinema and make its own way into the theatre. On one level, this decision lends weight to the point made by a number of critics that the film's representation of Estrella's memories includes events and incidents that she observed directly as well as events and incidents that she has only imagined. But it also undercuts this conclusion by affirming that these memories are just as much the property of another force, one that is so vividly depicted in *El espíritu de la colmena*: the cinema itself. The tendency of the camera to operate independently from the characters, the use of chiaroscuro lighting to illuminate small areas of the frame while keeping the rest in darkness, the slow fades that create the impression of watching scenes drawn from and receding into the darkness of the past: in *El Sur* these stylistic tropes signal that it is cinema—as much as the character—that is remembering.

This coincidence comes to the fore when the film pauses to contemplate the postcards that Estrella uses to construct her understanding of the South. Drawn from who-knows-where and jumbled together in a cigar box, the image of the South rendered in these postcards is one that, in the application of colour to what would have been black-and-white photographs, and in the staging of exoticised scenes of women dressed in mantillas, has been heavily worked over. The role of these *objets trouvés* is less about visualising what the South might look like and more to do with giving shape to the challenge that lies at the heart of the film: how to render the legacy of something that exceeds one's conscious knowledge, something that leaves its mark as a form of not-knowing.

How do we encounter this not-knowing? Primarily as a type of indetermination at the level of image and sound: What is it that I'm seeing? What might this strangely coloured image tell me about the enigmas that determine my experience of the past? In *El Sur* this indetermination marks the weight of a past that continues to press its claims on the present.

El Sur, dir. Víctor Erice, 1983

V

If the first part of *El Sur* concerns Estrella's attempts to understand the mystery of her father's past, the second part concerns the disillusionment that supersedes these attempts. 'I started wishing with all my heart that I could grow and suddenly be an adult so I could get far away from there,' Estrella's voiceover recalls about the crises that came to dominate her childhood. As if responding to this wish, a shot of Estrella as a child riding away from the house on her bicycle is dissolved into a shot taken from exactly the same position that reveals a now adolescent version of the character riding back towards the house. 'I grew up more or less like everyone else,' her voiceover recounts, 'getting used to being alone and to not thinking too much about happiness.' The change in her relationship to her father is summed up in a scene that echoes their previous encounter outside the town's cinema. This time it occurs outside a bar and, unlike the earlier encounter, the person Estrella observes from a distance is not shrouded in mystery but merely disoriented, someone who must call on the steady hand of a passerby to light his cigarette. The scene is about the changed relationship between father and daughter. But it is also about the continuation of Estrella's mirroring of aspects of her father's behaviour, as well as his obsession with phantoms. 'I never forgot Irene Ríos,' her voiceover tells us at the start of this scene. 'I kept looking for her on film posters. But I never saw her name again. It was as if the earth had swallowed her up.'

The denouement occurs one afternoon when Agustín picks up Estrella from school and takes her to lunch at the Grand Hotel. Apart from a wedding reception in an adjacent room, the restaurant is empty. Their conversation hints at familiar sources of contention—her relationship with the boy who refers to himself as El Carioco, Agustín's disapproval of her social life, his drinking. In the course of their conversation, she asks him a question that she has long wanted to ask: 'Who was Irene Ríos?' She then tells him about the night she saw his motorbike parked outside the cinema and followed him to the cafe, where she watched him write a letter. Rather than answering directly, Agustín dissembles. When he returns to the table after taking a few moments to splash water on his face, Estrella tells him that she has to go back to class. At this point Agustín's attention is grabbed by the sound of the paso doble that seeps into the restaurant from the adjoining room. It is the same paso doble that, earlier in the film, father and daughter danced on the day of her First Communion. Although Estrella can remember the day, it is clear from her response that this memory does not have the same impact as it does for her father. As she leaves the restaurant, Estrella pauses to peek through the curtains draped across the doors of the adjacent room at the bride and groom dancing. Rather than remaining with Estrella, the camera cranes up from her perspective to a position above the doors and gazes down at the wedding party through the transom window.

What are we being asked to remember at this moment? Most directly, it is the once-deep affection between father and daughter, embodied in their dance during the communion dinner. But the manner in which the camera cranes up from Estrella also prompts us to remember other moments in the film when the camera asserts its independence. The most affecting of these occurs during the dance between Agustín and Estrella. Beginning with a close-up of Estrella's communion veil draped over the back of an empty chair, the camera slowly tracks back to show us, first, the family members seated around the dinner table, and then father and daughter dancing together. After following their movements, the camera retraces its path, coming to rest again on the empty chair. We remember this action because it marks another moment when the camera's tendency to assert its independence gently distances us from the fiction. The intention is not to suspend the story. Rather, it is to enact an oscillation between two points of attention: the spectacle of the dance, and an insistent image of absence conveyed in the shot of the empty chair. One speaks of the present, the other of its inevitable passing away. One binds us to the story of Estrella's childhood, the other to the camera's role in telling this story.

'The camera may speak in the present,' Gilberto Perez reminds us, 'but it is a present now past when we watch it on the screen.' Its poignancy, he adds, is 'the poignancy of what reaches us from the past with the urgency of the present.' Perez's proposition helps to clarify what we are being asked to remember when the sound of the paso doble seeps into the restaurant. Once again, it is the cinema—this time, not as a particular place visualised in the story, or as an engagement with an unfinished childhood, but as a way of experiencing the present as always already past. This is the sad note carried into the restaurant during the afternoon when Estrella speaks to her father for the last time. We absorb this note as a memory about the cinema and its capacity to unsettle our place in the present.

Agustín (Omero Antonutti) and eight-year-old Estrella (Sonsoles Aranguren) dancing together during the Communion dinner. In *El Sur*, dir. Víctor Erice, 1983

From left, Agustín's mother, Rosario (Germaine Montero), and Milagros (Rafaela Aparicio). In *El Sur*, dir. Víctor Erice, 1983

VI

After Estrella leaves the restaurant, we observe Agustín sitting alone in the far corner of the restaurant, listening to the paso doble. The film then returns to the morning when Estrella discovers her father's pendulum underneath her pillow. Leaving Estrella propped on the edge of her bed, the film cuts to a long shot of the town's walls. When the camera cranes down from its perch, we catch sight of Agustín's body face down on the riverbank, his coat and rifle beside him. 'Before leaving the house,' Estrella's voiceover confides, 'he emptied his pockets. Among the things he left in a drawer was a small telephone receipt. That's how I found out that on the last night of his life my father had called the South. A number I didn't recognise.' In the closing moments, we see her slip this receipt—as well as the cigar box of postcards—into the suitcase that she will take with her on her journey to the South. 'The night before I left, I could hardly sleep,' her adult self recalls. 'Although I didn't show it, I was very nervous.' In the final shot, Estrella is standing directly in front of the camera, her gaze fixed on a point just to its right: 'At last I was going to see the South.'

This is the film's final shot only because the withdrawal of production funding meant that Erice was not able to film the last third of the script—the part that deals with Estrella's trip to the South. From various accounts of the details in the unfilmed portion of the script, it is easy enough to piece together how this material would have developed some of the threads left hanging in the story and, in particular, the nature of Agustín's relationship to Irene Ríos. The problem with this speculation is that it discounts an unfinishedness already there in the film's rendering of the South. Unfinishedness is not something that befalls the film, we might say: it is something that the film enables, both at the level of the events that define its story and the structures that it employs to tell this story. In their most powerful guise, this is what Erice's films do: they allow an engagement with experiences that, by their nature, must remain unrealised. Moreover, they locate these experiences at the heart of a larger reflection about the nature of cinema.

VII

For Erice, the cinema is where a stubborn silence becomes entangled in a compulsive puzzling over meaning. We go there not to reconstruct the past, but to look for signs of its current life. This understanding leads us back to our point of commencement: the director's own experiences as a cinemagoer. In *La morte rouge: soliloquio* (2006), the short film that he made as part of the exhibition *Correspondences: Víctor Erice and Abbas Kiarostami*, his voiceover recalls the dread evoked during a screening of Roy William Neill's murder-mystery *The Scarlet Claw* (1944). He remembers how this dread echoed in the 'atmosphere of a devastated society', and being struck by the silence of the adults around him in the cinema, all of whom seemed to be complicit in 'a secret that explained everything'. For Erice and his generation of cinemagoers, film both wounds and acts as a balm for the wounds: 'This double game of pain and consolation, of suffering and joy, that reached him from the screen, was the basis for his contradictory relationship with moving images.' In Erice's memory of cinema, we are undone by images and sounds and able to draw from this undoing a renewed encounter with what remains still be realised about the past.

6
'Together with Them We Are Also Alone'

I

James Agee concludes his biographical essay 'Knoxville: Summer 1915' by recalling the members of his family lying on quilts in the backyard of the family home. Mother, father, aunt and uncle. The author, too, can be found among these bodies. Night is drawing in. The hoses used by the neighbourhood men to water their lawns have been coiled and put away—the noise of their industry has been replaced by the rumble of automobiles on the street in front of the house and the thrum of locusts in the trees. In the penultimate paragraph, these sounds give way to the chatter of the people on the quilts as well as the sadness of finding oneself in two places, at once: *down here*, cocooned among the adult bodies gathered on the quilts, and already further on. 'By some chance, here they are, all on this earth; and who shall ever tell the sorrow of being on this earth, lying, on quilts, on the grass, in a summer evening, among the sounds of the night.' That the author has restored at least some of the particularities of this summer evening in Knoxville is cause for thanks: 'May God bless my people, my uncle, my aunt, my mother, my good father, oh, remember them kindly in their time of trouble; and in the hour of their taking away.'

The essay ends with the author being carried to bed, gently taking his leave from a place and a people whose affection provided protection and nurture, yet never entirely constituted who he was—or who he will become: 'Sleep, soft smiling, draws me unto her: and those receive me, who quietly treat me, as one familiar and well-beloved in that home: but will not, oh, will not, not now, not ever; but will not ever tell me who I am.'

In Agee's essay the experience of familial connection is not monumental, but precarious—or, better, time-bound. The bodies gathered on the quilts belong to a recognisable milieu; their habits are easy to identify. But they are also individuals who will never be seen again. The author wants us to notice these individuals, take in their singularities as well as their commonplace aspects, and, for as long as possible, *stay with them*—on this summer evening, on these quilts, on the grass.

II

'And it was all much more than I'm saying,' Richard Ford confesses near the start of his memoir *Between Them*. 'What I don't know can't rightly be called a feature of who he was. My father. Incomplete understanding of our parents' lives is not a condition of *their* lives. Only ours.' The idea that we might know our parents tends to strike us later in life. For a long time, we are content to view them as unremarkable parts of the landscape, rather than as individuals requiring our knowledge. The desire for knowledge, when it strikes, often coincides with the feeling of something being withheld: a vital detail that requires us to be more attentive, more aware of these people *as* people. Ford's novel *Wildlife*, for example, focuses on a period in a sixteen-year-old boy's life when he is forced to confront the cracks in his parents' marriage: his father's disorientation after losing his job as a golf pro at the local country club and sudden decision to volunteer to fight the fires raging in the mountains above the town, his mother's equally sudden affair with a local business identity, his father's failed attempt at revenge by setting fire to his rival's house. Without any siblings or close friends to provide some perspective, the narrator must grapple with the significance of these events on his own. The outcome is not an understanding of the motivations driving his parents' actions, but a bruised acceptance that adulthood involves finding ways to accommodate all that one doesn't know—about oneself as well as about others.

This recognition of not-knowing is central to *Between Them*. 'If anything, to realize you know less than all is respectful,' the author claims near the start, 'since children narrow the frame of everything they're a part of. Whereas being ignorant or only able to speculate about another's life frees that life to be more what it truly was.' The implications of this ignorance are registered in the author's reflections on his father. The basic details of Parker Ford's life are clear enough. Born to an Irish immigrant mother and a father who suicided when Parker was just twelve, he began his working life as a 'produce man' at a grocery store in Hot Springs, Arkansas. In his early twenties he met and married Edna Atkin, who was seventeen and living with her parents. His life after marrying Edna was structured around his job as a travelling salesman for the Faultless Starch Company, spending great stretches of time on the road, servicing the needs of businesses. The saving grace was that, with no children to worry about, his wife was happy to accompany him on these travels.

In the essay on his father, and the accompanying reflection on his mother's life that was written fifteen years earlier, Ford conjures a rich sense of the young couple's life together, mixing business with pleasure, establishing friendships with other salespeople and, as a result of the long hours in the car, getting to know each other in a way that is less common than one might imagine. This went on well into his father's thirties. Parenthood was not exactly a shock, but for a couple whose life had been defined by the absence of children it required some getting used to.

For a time after the author's birth, the old life of husband and wife on the road continued, only coming to an end when their young son's needs for a stable environment became impossible to ignore. Now, it was just Parker leaving the house on Monday morning, calling on the businesses that made up his designated territory, eating meals alone or with other salespeople, each night sleeping in a different hotel room, returning to the family's duplex on Congress Street in

Jackson, Mississippi, late on a Friday evening, spending the weekend catching up with his young family, resting, then setting out again on Monday morning. 'He knew he was mostly absent,' Ford intuits about his father's understanding of his life at this time. 'He knew she was looking after their life and me, and that it was complex for her. He *was* a presence, if not a father precisely. And he was her husband, the man she loved and waited for. It was acceptable.' Ford is careful neither to overdramatise nor underplay the effect of his father's absences. Seeing one's father only on weekends, and in an atmosphere where lingering conflicts needed to be carefully tamped down, was not normal. But neither was it tragic. 'My recalled feelings over that time—my little-boy life, in Jackson, on Congress, in my first years, in the forties and beginning fifties—are of a hectic, changing, provisional existence. They loved me, protected me. But the experience of life was of *events*, of things and people in motion, and of being often alone and to the side of things.'

In 1948 Parker Ford suffered his first heart attack. The author remembers visiting his ailing father in the hospital. 'Everything changed on that night,' he acknowledges. But it's also clear from his account of the last twelve years of his father's life that, on another level, nothing changed. The absences and time away from home that defined his father's life continued. The only difference now was that they were viewed in the context of the author's progression into adolescence and all the noise and distractions that accompany this time in a young person's life. Not surprisingly, he confesses to a haziness about certain details, as well as thinking that his father's absence was simply how life was to be lived. 'He was not a stranger,' he clarifies, 'but he was *like* a stranger, and while it was foregone that he loved me, it's possible he looked upon me the way I looked upon him.'

Partly to give this hazy figure some clarity, Ford lists all the fatherly things that Parker couldn't do: reliably start a lawnmower, properly hang a punching bag, erect a basketball backboard, operate a rotary barbecue, string up a hammock. To square the ledger, he recalls his father accompanying him and his mother to the hospital when he had to have his tonsils and adenoids removed, purchasing an array of short-lived pets, taking him to the occasional high-school football game. And from all this tallying of poorly recollected details we obtain a portrait of a father who was as 'good as he could be', and whose enduring lesson to his son involved a type of non-heroic resilience. 'I could not have said it at the time, but an unspoken part of my awareness must've been that I was the only son of a man who was trying to conduct life against odds. I can only intuit what was his *effect* on me. But if I had to I would say that because I was his son, I can recognize now that life is short and has inadequacies, that once again it requires crucial avoidances as well as fillings-in to be acceptable.'

In these passages Ford is doing something whose difficulty is belied by the directness of his writing: imbuing the foibles and particularities of an ordinary life, a life that would otherwise be considered unremarkable, with depth and dimension, while remaining faithful to what was, for him, its truest quality: not its lack of grandeur, but its unknowability. All lives have their secrets, that part that is turned away from us. The challenge for the writer is: how to keep faith with this?

In *Between Them* an inflection in the writing turns our attention back to the author, his partiality, his necessarily limited recollections and attempts to do justice to a figure who constantly escapes his grasp. The type of writing that emerges conforms to the tropes of a memoir, but one that gains its force from the author's determination to hold onto the condition of not-knowing, as if this might restore to his father's life a dimension taken away by the circumstances of his death. Never spelt out as such, not-knowing can be considered a form of responsibility that binds the author to those legacies he can neither accommodate nor abjure. 'Memory has pushed him further and further away until I "see" him—in those early days—as a large, smiling man standing on the other side of a barrier made of air, looking at me, possibly looking *for* me, recognizing me as his son but never coming quite close enough for me to touch.'

III

Parker Ford's death at the relatively early age of 55 took away the author's chance to forge a relationship with his father as an adult. But it also provided him with an important freedom. 'His sudden departure, the great, unjust loss of his life, handed me a life to live by my own designs, freed me to my own decisions. A boy could do worse than to lose his father—even a good father—just when the world begins to array itself all around him.' The impact of Parker's death is most profoundly registered on Edna's life. In the essay on his mother, the author confesses to knowing very little about her childhood in the north-west corner of Arkansas. The details that he is able to glean— her father's death from cancer sometime in the 1930s, her mother's remarriage to a much younger man, her time living in a Catholic boarding school, her unhappy post-school life being passed off by her mother as her younger sister and put to work as a cashier in the cigar stand at the Arlington Hotel in Hot Springs—create a picture of a time when options were limited and kindness was in short supply. 'For my mother, history was just small business, forgettable residues—some of them mean. Nothing in her past was heroic or edifying. The Depression—hard times all around—had something to do with that.'

Married life marked the commencement of better times: 'Drinking. Cars. Restaurants. Dancing. People they liked on the road. A life in the south. A swirling thing that didn't really have a place it was going.' The author's birth solidified this swirling, undirected thing into two distinct roles—Edna at home, looking after Richard; Parker away during the week, working. 'Life was going this way now and not that way anymore. They loved each other. They loved me. Nothing else much mattered.' This sense of a life proceeding according to its own volition, without much in the way of reflection, is punctuated by two memories that indicate the emergence in the young author's mind of a sharper, more differentiated sense of his mother as a person. The first involves the time when six-year-old Richard's disruptive behaviour drove his mother to run away, leaving him alone in the front yard of their house. 'I've never known how serious she was about needing to escape. Eventually she came back. But I have always understood from this event that there might be reasons to run away. In her case—alone, with a small child, in a strange city, knowing no one. That could be enough.' The memory of Edna's flight counterpoints another memory from around the same time—one that, on the surface, is far less dramatic. It involves the young author being accosted on the sidewalk by an elderly female neighbour, who asks him who he is. In response to being told that his name is Richard Ford, the neighbour replies: 'Oh, yes. Your mother's the cute little black-haired woman up the street.' The neighbour's words made such an impression because of the distance they established in his conception of his mother. The person evoked in the neighbour's description—'cute', 'little', 'black-haired'—is still *his* mother. But now she is also someone else: someone whose visibility to others marks a point of difference that must be accommodated in his sense of her personhood.

The author's recollection of this rupture draws attention to a distinctive dimension of the intimacy that bound him to his mother: 'This is the one quality of our lives with our parents that is often overlooked, and so devalued,' Ford declares at the start of his essay on Edna's life. 'Our parents intimately link us, closeted as we are in our lives, to a thing we're not, forging a joined separateness and a useful mystery, so that even together with them we are also alone.' Here it is again: not-knowing not as something lacking, but as the touchstone for our most intimate relationships. That we can be bound to a person in this way is a source of both comfort and an experience of alterity that runs through the history of the author's relationship to his mother.

Leaving home, going to college, finding his way as a writer, meeting the woman who would become his wife: so much of what defined his life took place after his father's passing. For Edna, on the other hand, the years after Parker's death were about finding ways to re-engage with a life that had lost something crucial. Getting various jobs, starting a short-lived relationship with a married man, taking care of her housebound mother, embarking on trips to California and Mexico. Through all these ups and downs, mother and son maintain a genuine intimacy. They *were* mother and son, after all. But they also enjoyed each other's company. This meant that Edna's regular visits to wherever Richard was living were always welcome. 'To visit us she arrived on trains and planes and in cars, ready to take us to dinner but also to loan us money. To have a room painted. Buy tires for our car. Pay a doctor bill. To worry about me. To listen. To be present for a little while as a part of what passed for our family—wherever we were—and then to go home.' But hanging over these comings and goings was a persistent sense of something not right that the author struggles to parse—some deep unhappiness in his mother that also cast its shadow over him.

No doubt this had to do with the hole in Edna's life left by the death of her husband: her inability to conceive of life without him as anything other than never completely right. Running alongside this was the realisation that the comings and goings that bound her to her son were the entirety of their life together. Ford is careful not to overstate his mother's unhappiness. But neither does he gloss over the extent to which her aloneness dominated her thinking about herself. He relays an anecdote told to him by his mother of being asked by a new acquaintance if she has any children: 'And without thinking she had said, "No." And then she'd thought to herself, *Oh, for God's sake. Of course I do. There's Richard.*' The author does not comment on Edna's motivations for telling him such a story, preferring to let it stand as a pointer to what he means when he describes the comings and goings that defined their life together as 'not a full enough *outcome*'. That no matter how many times she'd visit him or he'd visit her, they would not be able to overcome the aloneness that was their life together.

'I do not have my child,' the philosopher Emmanuel Levinas writes about the relationship between parent and child. 'I am my child.' Paternity, he insists, 'is a relation with a stranger who while being Other... *is* me, a relation of the I with a self which yet is not me.' To be true to Ford's account of his relationship with Edna, we need to switch their roles around and locate the author in the position of the parent and his mother as the child. But this does not diminish what is of value here for understanding the complex feelings of connection and estrangement that defined their relationship. His attempts to fathom her unhappiness and compensate for the hole left by Parker's death mark the point in their relationship when there is a continuation of an original dynamic and the commencement of a form of paternity that is not biological but ethical. Parker's death meant that the author had to take responsibility for Edna's happiness as well as her grief, without ever being in possession of this happiness or grief. Together with her, he remained alone.

IV

'And that is the way life went on. Not pointlessly. But not pointedly, either. Maybe this is also usual in our lives with our older parents—a feeling that some goal is being sought, and then the recognition of what that goal inevitably is, after which we return our attention to what's present now.' In 1973 Edna Ford was diagnosed with breast cancer. The removal of a breast and a course of radiotherapy gave her another seven years of life, a period characterised by great worry, agonised mental preparation and practical adjustments in both their lives. During the period of remission, at least, the pleasures to be had in later life were seized with greater firmness: cruises, visits to Hawaii, the forging of new friendships. 'Every year there was good news delivered, after worrying. And every year there was a time to celebrate and feel a reprieve.' Throughout this period, the author continued to live far away from his mother, relying on telephone calls and regular visits to assuage his anxieties and reassure himself that, despite everything, his mother was still all right.

In September 1981 Edna's cancer returned. The commencement of blood transfusions triggered an uptick in her general health, and by early October she was well enough to travel to Vermont to stay with her son and his partner. During this time, she watched TV, read books, went on country drives with her son, looked at antiques. Even in a time of dying, the author observes, there is still a life to be lived. The point came when Edna's incapacity necessitated a discussion about how long they could continue with such an arrangement. The author's recollection of this conversation turns on a small but irrevocable moment of deferral on his part, when, after telling his mother that she should just move in with him and witnessing the relief that this sparked, he immediately cautions that it might be best for them to wait and see if there is an improvement in her condition. Nothing terrible in this caveat. But it was enough to push his mother away. Looking back, he is unsure what drove him to say this. Was he wary of the imposition? Or was he clinging to the possibility of his mother's ongoing life? Or was it some other impulse, triggered by her death being so near, so proximate to him? 'I'll never be sure,' he admits. 'But the truth is that anything we ever could've done for each other after that, passed by in those moments and was gone. Even together we were once again alone.'

The pain associated with this recollection has its roots in Edna's vulnerability; at the same time, it affirms that not-knowing is not a matter of something that is out there, but of forces that lie deep within. To put this more plainly, Edna is no hazy figure glimpsed from the other side of a barrier made of air. She is someone whose happiness and grief impose themselves on her son's solitude. 'My mother and I look alike,' he tells us immediately after his account of Edna's death. 'Full, high forehead. Same chin, same nose. There are pictures to show it. In myself I see her, hear her laugh in mine.' The resemblance that the author identifies here is a matter of something larger than shared physical characteristics: it is an acknowledgement of his life as a consequence of hers.

He concludes his reflection on Edna's life with an account of what their relationship made possible—what she helped him to know, fully and without doubt: 'She made possible for me my truest affections, as an act of great literature bestows upon its devoted reader. And I have known that moment with her we would all like to know, the moment of saying, *Yes. This is what it is.* An act of knowing that confirms life's finality and truest worth. I have known that.'

V

'Our parents' lives, even those enfolded in obscurity,' Ford writes in the Afterword, 'offer us our first, strong assurance that human events have consequence. *Here we are*, after all. The future is unpredictable and hazardous, but our parents' lives both enact us and help distinguish us.' In *Between Them* the attribution of consequence occurs hand in hand with a recognition of its counterforce: that the type of life lived by his parents is one whose most natural state is to pass without consequence or comment. His touchstone for this recognition is W. H. Auden's poem 'Musée des Beaux Arts', which takes as its subject Bruegel's painting *Landscape with the Fall of Icarus* or, more specifically, that small portion in the bottom right-hand corner of the painting in which the upturned body of Icarus is depicted disappearing into the water, unnoticed by the various figures nearby, the most prominent of whom is the ploughman, shown busy at work. 'The ploughman may / Have heard the splash, the forsaken cry,' Auden muses. 'But for him it was not an important failure.'

Landscape with the Fall of Icarus, Pieter Bruegel the Elder, c. 1560

The enduring truth rendered in the poem and Bruegel's painting informs Ford's own writings, and Agee's lamentations at the end of 'Knoxville: Summer, 1915': 'The world often doesn't notice us.' How does one write about this lack of notice, this transience, without turning it into something it is not? In Agee's biographical essay, it involves being attentive to the sounds of the long-past summer evenings in Knoxville: the thrum of the locusts, the clopping of the horses' hoofs as they hit the asphalt in front of the house, the 'iron whine' of automobiles as they gather speed and disappear into the distance and the different registers of tone and pitch generated by the water streaming through the hoses wielded by the neighbourhood men. It involves placing these sounds in their proper context: time's passing.

In Ford's memoir, this challenge is inseparable from his feelings of longing for his parents: 'In difficult moments, long after their deaths, I often experience the purest longing for them—for their actuality. So, to write about them, to *not* turn away, is not only a means to remedy my longing by imagining them near, but is also to point toward that actuality, which—once again—is where my understanding of importance begins.' In the essay on Parker, staying close to actuality is registered as a check on one's thoughts or, better, a realisation that what wasn't grasped about a situation might well be its truest dimension. In the essay on Edna, adhering to actuality is connected to the less obvious idea that the intimacy of our deepest relationships is forged by separation. It is about recognising how this separation leaves its mark on us.

VII

Near the end of *Wildlife* the narrator looks back on his parents' life together after the end of his mother's brief affair and her return to the family home. He wonders what it was that made them believe that only by remaining together could they hold onto something important about themselves. 'I do not know exactly what that something was,' he admits. 'But that is how our life resumed after then, for the little time that I was at home. And for many years after that. They lived together—that was their life—and alone.' The only inkling appears earlier in the story, when, by way of an explanation for her sudden affair, his mother tells him: 'Your life doesn't mean what you have, sweetheart, or what you get. It's what you're willing to give up ... You have to give things up. That's the rule. It's the major rule for everything.' How we accommodate ourselves to an absence that is fundamental: this, rather than the bewildering events surrounding his parents' separation, is the book's central mystery, the matter that draws the narrator back to the past.

Nearly three decades later, Ford reflects on the absences, insufficiencies and frailties that writing the memoir has disclosed in him: 'When I turn to regard life—my own or others'—I now never fail to be struck, amid the onslaught of all that's happened and still is happening, by how much that's gone from me. Absences seem to surround and intrude upon everything.' He tempers the pathos of this statement by acknowledging that these absences cannot be viewed as a loss, merely as how life must be lived—'another enduring truth we must notice'. This, then, is the memoirist's task: to maintain faith with the rents and absences that determine our closest relationships, and to regard them not as defects but as the touchstones for everything we know and hold dear.

7
'A Poor and Precious Secret'

I

> I'm writing these pages in November 1996. It seldom stops raining. Tomorrow we shall be in December, and fifty-five years will have passed since Dora ran away. It gets dark early, and it's just as well: night obliterates the grayness and monotony of these rainy days when you wonder if it really is daytime, or if we are going through some intermediary stage, a sort of gloomy eclipse lasting till dusk. Then the street lamps and shop windows and cafés light up, the evening air freshens, contours sharpen, there are traffic jams at the crossroads and hurrying crowds in the streets. And in the midst of all these lights, all this hubbub, I can hardly believe that this is the city where Dora lived with her parents, where my father lived when he was twenty years younger than I am now. I feel as though I am alone in making the link between Paris then and Paris now, alone in remembering all these details. There are moments when the link is strained and in danger of snapping, and other evenings when the city of yesterday appears to me in fleeting gleams behind that of today.
>
> **Patrick Modiano,** *Dora Bruder*

Patrick Modiano's 1997 book *Dora Bruder* chronicles the author's investigation of the events leading to the deportation of a sixteen-year-old Jewish girl during the Nazi occupation of France. The trigger for this investigation is his perusal of a notice in an issue of *Paris-soir* dated 31 December 1941: 'Missing, a young girl, Dora Bruder, age 15, height 1 m 55, oval-shaped face, gray-brown eyes, gray sports jacket, maroon pullover, navy blue skirt and hat, brown gym shoes.' Anyone with information on the missing girl's whereabouts is requested to forward this information to M. and Mme Bruder, 41 Boulevard Ornano, Paris. In the eight years after reading this notice, he pieces together a history of the Bruder family—Ernest, Cécile and Dora—and their fate during the Occupation, when approximately 75,000 Jewish men, women and children were rounded up by the French police and sent to concentration camps in Germany and Nazi-occupied Poland.

From the records of the Catholic boarding school where Dora was sent by her parents, he discovers the date she was enrolled and the date she was recorded as missing: 9 May 1940 and 14 December 1941. From the police blotter at the Clignancourt police station he learns that almost two weeks passed before her father reported her disappearance. The family dossier kept by the Prefecture of Police reveals that, three months after filing this report, on 19 March 1942, Ernest Bruder is himself arrested and interned at Drancy, the holding camp for Jewish residents prior to their deportation to Auschwitz. Dora next appears in the official police paperwork a month later: she is once again residing with her mother at 41 Boulevard Ornano. But the reunion is temporary. Papers belonging to the former Union générale des israélites de France confirm that she ran away a second time. The final part of the chronology is the discovery of Dora's name on the register of the Tourelles internment centre, her transfer to Drancy on 13 August 1942 and, just over a month later, her departure on a convoy of trains headed for Auschwitz.

Modiano's careful documentation of these events is an indictment of the measures adopted by the French authorities to support the genocidal policies of the German occupiers. But to understand the nature of his achievement we need to consider how his method distances itself from the procedures of traditional historiography. Modiano's book commemorates the lives lost during the dark years of the Occupation and alerts us to what remains still to be said about these lives. The description of the incessant November rain and the grey monotony of the shortened days that conjure a gloomy eclipse suggests an interplay between memory and its obliteration that is central to the book's rendition of Dora's past, as well as the author's troubled relationship with his own father.

II

In 'On the Concept of History' Walter Benjamin counters the definition of the historian's task identified by the nineteenth-century German historian Leopold von Ranke. He insists that 'articulating the past historically does not mean recognising it "the way it really was." It means appropriating a memory as it flashes up in a moment of danger.' Modiano's method shares with Benjamin's recasting of the historian's labour an emphasis on seizing moments of correspondence between the past and the present that would otherwise have fallen prey to the ever present forces of amnesia. The precarious nature of this correspondence comes to the fore when Modiano visits the hotels where the Bruder family lived. Instead of some trace of their habitation, the overwhelming impression is of emptiness. Part of the difficulty, he reasons, is that Dora's parents emigrated to Paris: her father from Vienna, via a stint in the French Foreign Legion; her mother and her family as Jewish refugees from Budapest. 'They are the sort of people who leave few traces. Virtually anonymous. Inseparable from those Paris streets, those suburban landscapes where, by chance, I discovered that they had lived.'

In order not to lose sight of his subject, Modiano interpolates his own memories of the neighbourhoods where Dora lived with her family. 'As a child, she would have played in the Square Clignancourt ... In the evenings, the neighbors would place their chairs outside and sit on the sidewalk for a chat. Or take a lemonade together on the café terrace. Sometimes men who could have been either real goatherds or else peddlers from the fairs would come by with a few goats and sell you tall glasses of milk for almost nothing. The froth gave you a white mustache.' The image of the frothy residue works in counterpoint to the historical forces that, over time, strip these memories of their footings. In the same passage the author recalls that nearby, at the Porte de Clignancourt, was a district of ramshackle dwellings and warehouses. Encountering this vanished landscape in photographs, he experiences for the first time the feeling of 'emptiness that comes with the knowledge of what has been destroyed, razed to the ground'.

The boulevards and streets where the author looks for traces of Dora's existence mark the obliteration of what has come before—the people and histories that claimed these boulevards and streets as their own—and the place where this obliteration awaits its redemption. This possibility requires certain things of the author. 'It took me four years to discover her exact date of birth,' he admits. 'And a further two years to find out her place of birth: Paris, 12th arrondissement. But I am a patient man. I can wait for hours in the rain.' The other requirement brings us closer to what is distinctive about his method: clairvoyance. Rather than a gift, clairvoyance is part and parcel of the writer's profession: 'The imaginative leaps this requires, the need to fix your mind on points of detail—to the point of obsession, in fact—so as not to lose the thread and give in to natural laziness.' The purpose of this obsessive attentiveness is twofold: to oppose the powerful forces of erasure that never stop shaping our engagement with the past, and to disrupt our relationship to the present.

Built into Modiano's characterisation of the writer as seer is an acute investment in images. Near the start of the book, he describes a handful of photographs of Dora and the members of her family. 'They are seated, their elbows resting on a sort of pedestal,' he observes about a shot of her parents on their wedding day. 'She is enveloped in a long white veil that trails to the floor and seems to be knotted at her left ear. He wears tails with a white bow tie.' In the next photograph, Dora is standing between Cécile and Ernest. She couldn't be more than two years old, he speculates. Another photograph shows her a decade older, holding a book in her right hand. An oval-shaped head-and-shoulder photograph reveals Dora—slightly older, still—between her mother and father: 'All three are in single file, their faces turned toward the camera: first, Dora and her mother, both in white blouses, then Ernest Bruder, in jacket and tie.'

The approximate age of the figures, their items of clothing and postures, as well as the props and background elements: this is as far as he will go in his interpretation of the photographs. The one exception occurs later in the book when he describes a photo of Dora standing alongside her mother and grandmother. The photo was taken either in 1941, when Dora was enrolled in the Catholic boarding school, or in the spring of 1942, after the police had returned her to the family home and prior to her second disappearance. After describing the arrangement of the three women and the details of their clothing, he considers Dora's facial expression: 'She holds her head high, her eyes are grave, but a smile is beginning to float about her lips. And this gives her face an expression of sad sweetness and defiance.' The rest of the paragraph is concerned with whether Ernest Bruder's absence from the photograph indicates that he had already been arrested and whether the skirt Dora is wearing is the same navy-blue skirt mentioned in the missing-person notice. 'In any case,' he concludes, 'it would seem that the three women have put on their Sunday best to face this anonymous lens.'

Dora Bruder with her grandmother and mother

107

For Modiano, the anonymous lens situates everything on an equal footing: clothing, hairstyles, elements of decor, bodily postures, facial expressions. In this view of things, Dora's blouse with a white collar has the same importance as the expression on her face or what this expression might reveal about her situation. This levelling of significance draws out a tension central to the author's writing, between the fleeting details of human existence and the capacity of memory to establish a connection between past and present. The descriptions of the photographs are where human memory—characterised as under threat—intersects with the memoryless world of objects and things. Things may grab our attention. They may fascinate. But they are also nonessential. They pass into the inert realm occupied by yesterday's fashions and the dead.

III

Premier rendez-vous, dir. Henri Decoin, 1941

Near the book's midpoint, the author describes a feeling of unease that arose while he watched a film that, in the summer of 1941, was playing in Parisian cinemas: *Premier rendez-vous*, a French comedy starring Danielle Darrieux and Louis Jourdan. Perhaps Dora had seen the film, he wonders, and its story about a young girl who runs away from a boarding school had contributed to her own decision to run away. But after carefully scrutinising its sets and decor, he concludes that his feeling of unease stems from something else entirely: the film's burnishment by a form of light that destabilises the world on screen. 'Every image seemed veiled in an arctic whiteness that accentuated the contrasts and sometimes obliterated them. The lighting was at once too bright and too dim, either stifling the voices or making their timbre louder, more disturbing.' The extraordinary thing about this unnerving illumination is its point of origin:

> Suddenly, I realized that this film was impregnated with the gaze of moviegoers from the time of the Occupation—people from all walks of life, most of whom would not have survived the war. They had been taken out of themselves after having seen this film one Saturday night, their night out. While it lasted, you forgot the war and the menacing world outside. Huddled together in the dark of a cinema, you were caught up in the flow of images on the screen, and nothing more could happen to you. And, by some kind of chemical process, this combined gaze had materially altered the actual film, the lighting, the voices of the actors.

Modiano's account of the film can be situated alongside other writings on cinema that rely on notions of imprinting. Most famously, André Bazin asserts that photography and film stand apart from other types of images in their capacity to render an image that is 'more than a mere approximation, a kind of decal or transfer'. Looking for a suitable analogy, he turns to the authenticating force of the fingerprint. Elsewhere, he refers to the moulding of death masks. In *Dora Bruder* we also find a direct connection between cinema and the world. But whereas Bazin considers this connection from the point of view of the object situated in front of the camera's lens, Modiano prioritises the capacity of the images on screen to register the gaze of those who have been their audience. The process of imprinting is projected out into the auditorium, into the space between the images on screen and the spectators gathered together in front of these images. Fifty-five years later, the author encounters evidence of this imprinting in the arctic whiteness of the film's images and the disturbing timbre of its voices.

Between the situation of those viewers who watched the film during the dark nights of the Occupation and whose existence was swept away by the terrible forces massed against them, and the author's own situation in front of the same images many years later, we encounter a connection that is both highly speculative and grounded in the material qualities of images. The relationship to the past is marked by feelings of transience, as well as an unsettling proximity whose most overt manifestation is an extended rhetorical conceit. 'While it lasted, you forgot the war and the menacing world outside. Huddled together in the dark of a cinema, you were caught up in the flow of images on the screen, and nothing more could happen to you.' 'The "you" draws the reader back into the past, into Modiano's memories and Dora's story alike,' the scholar Susan Weiner explains. 'But the "you" also brings the past forward, a quasi-somatic experience for the reader. The "you" embodies our imagination, linking us to the familiarity of fear, solitude, and momentary freedom.'

True enough. But the author's use of 'you' does more than link our imagination to the experiences of those who did not survive the war: it lends these experiences a voice that the forces of history seem determined to erase. The rhetorical device that comes closest to encapsulating Modiano's achievement is prosopopoeia: that form of address in which a deceased or absent loved one is made to speak. To be sure, the use of 'you' maintains an element of indirectness in the address; at the same time, it exemplifies the paradox at the core of prosopopoeia's relationship to memorialisation: its form of address incorporates the presence of an absent other and, at the same time, marks the failure of this incorporation. We experience this paradox as an aporia, Jacques Derrida proposes: 'The aporia of mourning and of prosopopeia, where the possible remains impossible. Where *success fails*. And where faithful interiorization bears the other and constitutes him in me (in us), at once living and dead.'

Modiano's use of 'you' activates this aporiatic encounter that configures the other as both living and dead. In so doing, it confirms that clairvoyance is more than the harnessing of flashes of intuition. It is also about drawing from the encounter with images forms of historical engagement whose starting point is the finitude of human existence.

IV

In the book's closing section, Modiano details the routines and administrative procedures that governed the lives of those detained at Tourelles prior to their departure for Drancy: the morning roll call, the food served in the refectory at lunch, the location of the exercise yard, the process for arranging a visit ... We learn about the treatment of those detainees officially labelled 'Friends of Jews', who were also interned at the barracks and the overcrowding as the number of arrests rapidly increased. The piling up of information in these passages is how the author holds on to a level of detail about Dora's life at the point when the specific elements of this life threaten to disappear into a much larger history. But as is always the case in Modiano's writings, the pieces of information gesture to a connection that is always just out of reach. The more we are told about Dora's past and the events that determine her fate, the more we come face to face with an absence that is a constitutive part of her history.

The author's determination to maintain faith with this absence is reiterated in the closing lines, when he admits that he will never know how Dora spent her days on the run from the boarding school and her family, as well as from the police, whose only interest was to ensure that she could be made to disappear for good. 'That is her secret,' he insists. 'A poor and precious secret that not even the executioners, the decrees, the occupying authorities, the Dépôt, the barracks, the camps,

History, time—everything that defiles and destroys you—have been able to take away from her.'

In these concluding reflections, the questions that at the start of the book motivate the author's engagement with Dora's story—Why did she run away from the relative safety of the Catholic boarding school? How did she spend her time during those winter nights when she was on the run?—are no longer mysteries to be solved. Rather, they are the mark of an unknowability that enables Dora's history to wrest free of the forces that lay claim to its significance. Might this provide another way to describe the function of the image in Modiano's writing—as a means to remain faithful to a secret that has made its home in us?

'I go to the movies for entertainment,' Jean Louis Schefer declares at the start of *The Ordinary Man of Cinema*, 'but sometimes while I'm there I also accidentally learn something, something different from what the film teaches me.' This lesson concerns cinema's capacity to connect with memories and experiences lost to the erosions of time. These memories and experiences are the product of a 'private pact' between the cinema and 'an unexpressed part of ourselves: that part given over to silence and to a relative aphasia'. The cinema aligns these memories and experiences to the operation of visible forms—bodies, gestures and actions that conjure the uncertain relationship 'between visible things and a secret that would be simply their own'. The paradoxical nature of these secrets is that they demand to be written. For Schefer, the experience of cinema is also a writerly experience—an experience of what can and cannot be communicated through writing.

Likewise, in Modiano's moving tribute to the disappeared the extraordinary conceit that images can register the gaze of those who were their viewers is a powerful evocation of the labile nature of screen images; at the same time, it galvanises the feelings of mutuality that run through his book. If we are able to recall images from movies that we have watched, then is it not possible that these same images harbour the capacity to remember us—to remember aspects of our histories that we have forgotten or never known? This mutuality is characteristic of a larger tendency on the author's part to turn the whole of Paris into a space of memory, in which his search for clues about Dora's existence intersects with events and incidents that define his own past.

Like Dora, the author's father had no Jewish dossier number, and thus during the Occupation also occupied a kind of dangerous limbo. But unlike Dora, Albert Modiano was able to use his connections in the black market to escape the net cast by the police. The author's account of these correspondences insists on leaving a space for what cannot be known; equally, it frames the book's engagement with the past as premised on an obligation or debt that can never be defrayed.

Recounting the fate of Albert Schaky, a resistance fighter and novelist who once occupied the same bedroom in the apartment where Modiano lived as a child, he observes: 'Just before I was born, he and others like him had taken all the punishments meted out to them in order that we should suffer no more than pinpricks.' In *Dora Bruder* photography and cinema help us to understanding how this debt might be written—the figures of speech that encapsulate the image's unsettling historicity. The intense illumination that renders the images of *Premier rendez-vous* both too bright and too dim suggests the risks involved in such an endeavour. These are the same risks that Benjamin has in mind when he writes about our danger-filled engagement with images of the past: 'For it is an irretrievable image of the past which threatens to disappear in any present that does not recognize itself as intended in that image.' So much of the gravity that characterises Modiano's historical method is encapsulated in this injunction to see ourselves as *intended* in the image of the past. In *Dora Bruder* this injunction means at least two things: that we are duty bound to give the image a legibility that time, habit and the operations of official history are determined to erase, and that in rendering the image legible our own histories have become implicated. In this encounter with the precariousness of the past, something of our own time and place threatens to disappear.

V

The narrator of Modiano's novella *Afterimage* recounts his friendship with a photographer named Francis Jansen, an Italian national born in Antwerp who spent the first two years of the Occupation in Paris working for the illustrated news magazine *Tempo*. Like Dora, Jansen is rounded up and interned at Drancy. After his connections in the Italian consulate manage to secure his release, he visits an address given to him by a friend and fellow inmate. On his initial visit, he is unable to find any trace of his friend's family or girlfriend. Following the liberation of Paris he returns to the same address, only to again come away empty-handed. To counter his feelings of helplessness, he photographs the surrounding buildings and courtyard. Even if the people who once lived here have disappeared, he reasons, the images will preserve the places where they lived. Many years later and after Jansen himself has disappeared, the narrator gazes at these images in a book of his photographs. The images of the buildings and courtyard bathed in summer sun confirm not the preservation of what is no longer, he is forced to admit, but an irremediable feeling of loss. This feeling culminates one afternoon when he pauses to catch his breath on a park bench. 'I was going to disappear in this garden, amid the Easter Monday crowds. I was losing my memory and couldn't understand French anymore ... The efforts I'd made for thirty years to have a trade, give my life some coherence, try to speak and write a language as best I could so as to be certain of my nationality—all that tension suddenly released. It was over. I was nothing now.'

In *Dora Bruder* the grey November evenings when the illumination of the street lamps and shop windows and the hubbub of the crowds in the streets set the author's mind to the link between Paris then and Paris now conjure a similar feeling of dissolution. Near the end of the book, Modiano recounts a weekend visit to the Tourelles barracks where Dora was interned with other Jewish residents. 'On that particular Sunday, the boulevard was empty, lost in a silence so deep that I could hear the rustling of the plane trees.' As he follows the line of the high perimeter wall surrounding the still standing buildings he notices a sign, affixed to the wall, that identifies the site as a Military

Zone: 'Filming or Photography Prohibited.' 'I told myself that nobody remembers anything anymore. Behind the wall there lay a no-man's-land, a zone of emptiness and oblivion ... And yet, from time to time, beneath this thick layer of amnesia, you can certainly sense something, an echo, distant, muted, but of what, precisely, it is impossible to say.' In the end, *Dora Bruder* is not about cinema or photography. Rather, it is about the experiences that they enable—experiences of loss, as well as an unsettling proximity to people and events whose histories demand something of us. The distinctive nature of this demand lies in its injunction that we acknowledge the right of the other to flee the safety of whatever shelter has been provided, yet also endeavour to ensure that those who have been the victims of history are not abandoned to the forces of erasure. This obligation conjures a scenario where, at each point in the creation and circulation of images of the past, a trace is registered, a connection forged whose precariousness places in question our ability to know the present.

Photography and cinema as ways of understanding the beckonings of history: Modiano is certainly not the first to pursue this connection. His achievement is to use these beckonings to test the limits of what can and cannot be communicated through writing. Perhaps what *Dora Bruder* allows us to conceive of is a form of writing operating at the intersection of fiction, memoir and cultural history, in which the objective is to mark our inhabitation by images, stories and secrets that are not ours to own. The obligation borne by this form of writing is not one of exposition or unveiling, but of maintenance: holding on to what cannot be known about the past. In *Dora Bruder*, the image takes us closer to a limit. 'Like finding yourself on the edge of a magnetic field,' the author observes during his visit to Tourelles, 'with no pendulum to pick up the radiation.'

8
'A Light from Before'

I

'All the images will disappear,' Annie Ernaux writes at the start of her third-person memoir, *The Years*. She then lists some of these images, the ones located at the front of mind, at least. Images of places, sensations and experiences. Images that constitute the memory of historical events, newspaper headlines, films watched, books read, as well as behaviours and attitudes that stamped her past. Images brought to life in short bursts of writing that intensify the details recalled. Images, finally, that will vanish along with the person endeavouring to recall their provenance and impact. We are talking about images, remember. They belong as much to the complex paths of memory as they do to the world outside.

But if these images are destined to disappear, they also animate a desire to develop a form of writing that can resist this disappearance. In Ernaux's memoir this involves drawing from images a collective dimension, while also locating them as part of an individual history experienced in two ways, simultaneously: as the chronological unfolding of one year after the next and as moments of coexistence. Standing in line at the supermarket, she becomes aware of all the other times in her life when she has been in a similar position. Looking around at the other women, she imagines that they are different renditions of herself, 'taken apart and separated like matryochka dolls. She pictures herself here in ten or fifteen years with a cart filled with sweets and toys for grandchildren not yet born. But she sees that woman as improbable, just as the girl of twenty-five saw the woman of forty.' From this sensation, she sketches the outlines of a project in which these coexisting images of herself are assembled to form an account of her own history, from birth during the Second World War up to the present, that would double as a history of her generation.

'Each time she begins, she meets the same obstacles: how to represent the passage of historical time, the changing of things, ideas, and manners, and the private life of this woman?' Faced with this challenge, she replaces the personal pronoun 'I' with the impersonal pronoun 'she', creating the impression of pursuing her history as if it were the history of someone else. Someone with whom she is intimately acquainted. She also employs another device: written descriptions of photographs, starting with a photo in an oval frame of a fat baby with pouty lips and moving through to a photo of a middle-aged woman cuddling a little girl in a manner that suggests the familial connection between grandmother and granddaughter. The photographs, she proposes near the book's conclusion, will capture 'the successive body shapes and social positions of her being—freeze-frames on memories, and at the same time reports on the development of her existence, the things that have made it singular, not because of the nature of the elements of her life ... but because of their combinations, each unique unto itself. To this "incessantly other" of photos will correspond, in mirror image, the "she" of writing.'

II

The descriptions of the photographs facilitate the step away from 'I' to 'she'. At the same time, they provide the context for something else central to Ernaux's memoir: the transmission of light. Not far into the memoir she describes a black-and-white photograph of two girls standing on a garden path, 'shoulder to shoulder, arms folded behind their backs. Behind them, flowering shrubs and a high brick wall'. On the back of the photo: '*July 1955, St. Michel Convent School grounds.*' The author fills in the circumstances surrounding the taking of the photo: for example, that both girls removed their school smocks before the photo was taken; that the curls on the shorter girl with brunette hair and glasses are the result of a perm that, since her Holy Communion, has become a May ritual, and that this girl is the same one who in an earlier photo taken on a beach can be seen wearing pigtails. Nothing in the image definitively locates it as occurring when it does, smack in the middle of the middle year of the 1950s. For the writer, however—the one who encounters herself draped in its details and looking back at its circumstances—it provides an unmistakable link to a moment in time: 'The beam that lights one side of the girl's face and the jumper, between the breasts, was for her a sensation of heat from the June sun of a year that no historian, or anyone else who lived at the time, could mistake for any other than 1955.'

How do we make sense of this light? What role does it play in the writer's struggle to represent the passage of historical time, while also lending a voice to the private life of a woman? A place to begin is that split second in the summer of 1955 when the illumination cast by the two young girls standing in front of the flowering shrubs passed through the camera's lens and left its imprint on the film emulsion. Many years later, the image produced conjures the heat of that long ago summer: light as a moment of contact that brings the past into the present. André Bazin sums up the disquiet that accompanies this moment when he describes the snapshots gathered in family albums as 'the disturbing presence of lives halted at a set moment in their duration, freed from their destiny; not, however, by the prestige of art but by the power of an impassive mechanical process'.

In *The Years* this disturbance coincides with the author's evocation of a particular social world. Recalling the lives of her forebears in the Normandy region of France, she concludes that memory was handed down not through stories but bodily attitudes: 'The ways of walking, sitting, talking, laughing, eating, hailing someone, grabbing hold of objects. It passed body to body, over the years, from the remotest countrysides of France and other parts of Europe: a heritage ... lying beyond individual difference and the gaps between the goodness of some and the wickedness of others.' For these people, memory was 'eating noisily and displaying the progressive metamorphosis of food in the open mouth, wiping one's lips with a piece of bread, mopping the gravy from a plate so thoroughly that it could be put away without washing, tapping the spoon on the bottom of the bowl, stretching at the end of dinner.'

Incarnated in the actions of her parents and her parents' parents, light is a moment of recognition that allows her to measure a distance—between the past and the present, between the person she was then and the person she is now. The descriptions of the photographs are where this distance allows itself to be seen. Another photograph of the same girl shows her standing in a sunny courtyard. Once again, the writing details a stage in her physical development. 'Other than the cheekbones and the shape of the breasts, now more developed, there is nothing to remind us of the girl with glasses of two years ago ... At the precise moment when she smiles, she is probably thinking only of herself, of this photo of herself gazing at the new girl she feels herself becoming.' Along with the bodily changes that accompany adolescence, the thing that distinguishes this girl from the one in the earlier photos is her awareness of her status as lower down the social scale than her classmates. 'Her family doesn't have a fridge or a bathroom,' we are informed, 'the lavatories are at the back of the courtyard and she still hasn't been to Paris.'

Social standing also figures in the description of a black-and-white photograph of three girls and a boy that bears the inscription 'University Campus. Mont-Saint-Aignam. June '63. Brigitte, Alain, Annie, Gérald, Annie, Ferrid.' The girl we saw in the previous photos has dispensed with the glasses and become more womanly. The photo was taken at 'a time of sleepless nights, long discussions in bars, rented rooms in town, caresses on naked skin, on the verge of reckless, to the strains of *La Javanaise*'. This was also a time when she felt cut adrift—not just from the bourgeois world of her classmates, but also the working-class world of her parents. 'She has gone over to the other side, but she cannot say of what. The life behind her is made up of disjointed images. She feels she is nowhere, "inside" nothing except knowledge and literature.'

Her attainment of university qualifications and marriage to a man from an educated family, the birth of their two children, the divorce whose circumstances are left undisclosed, the taking of lovers, the crisis in her health, the death of her parents and attempts to support her two sons through their own struggles: these milestones map the shift from the working-class world of her parents to the middle-class respectability of life as a university teacher living on the outskirts of Paris. They also conjure the coexisting images of a person that the memoir locates as part of the collective history of postwar France. Incarnated in the author's interactions with others, light is how this history is lived and retained at a bodily level. It is how she appear to others and how others appear to her.

III

A Man's Place, Ernaux's book about her father's life, begins with the near coincidence of two moments: her passing the test to qualify for the secondary teachers' training certificate and, two months later, the death of her father at the age of 67. The opening pages detail the events immediately following his death: the cleaning and laying out of the body, the funeral arrangements, the respect shown by the regulars at her parents' cafe. During the train journey home to Paris, she tries to prevent her young son from disturbing the other passengers in the first-class carriage: 'I suddenly realized with astonishment: "Now I really am bourgeois," and "It's too late."' The realisation triggers a desire to explain the transformation: 'To write about my father, his life and the distance which had come between us during adolescence. Although it had something to do with class, it was different, indefinable. Like fractured love.' She commences work on a novel. Halfway through, she is overwhelmed by feelings of disgust: 'I realize now that a novel is out of the question. In order to tell the story of a life governed by necessity, I have no right to adopt an artistic approach

... I shall collate my father's words, tastes and mannerisms, the main events of his life, all the external evidence of his existence.'

The first half of the book outlines the history of her father's parents, who worked for wealthy farmers and lived in a small cottage with beaten-earth floors. She scrutinises the pages of his primary-school reader, and draws out odd phrases and moral imperatives: *'One should learn always to be content with one's lot'; 'Charity towards the poor is the most precious thing in the world.'* She recounts his life as a farm labourer in the period between the world wars, and the circumstances surrounding his meeting of the woman he would marry and with whom he would escape the impoverishment of their working-class lives by saving their money to purchase a small cafe. She relays the resentments of relatives who saw their modest success as a betrayal. The worry that keeps returning is that this gathering of external evidence gives life not to her father, but someone who is a product of the book's structure. 'If on the other hand I indulge in personal reminiscences, I remember him as he was ... and I forget about everything that ties him to his own social class. Each time I face this dilemma I have to tear myself from the subjective point of view.'

Her solution forecasts the role played by photographs in *The Years*. In the book on her father's life, the first photograph described shows him in the backyard of the family home: 'A white shirt with rolled-up sleeves, a pair of trousers, flannels most likely, sloping shoulders and slightly rounded arms. An expression of discontent on his face, maybe he wasn't quite ready for the photograph ... Nothing in the picture to account for the past suffering, or his future hopes. Just the obvious signs of age—a slight paunch, the black hair beginning to recede—and those, more discreet, of his social condition: his arms hanging stiffly at his sides; the washhouse and lavatory in the background.' These descriptions anchor her father's life within a particular milieu. They also prise apart two moments that lend the viewing of a photograph its feelings of discontinuity: the moment recorded in the photograph and the present moment of looking. In Ernaux's writing this does not happen all at once. Rather, it emerges through the accretion of surface details that reveal the conditions which determined her father's life and point to all that remains unresolved in her relationship to this life. The details are just details. But they are also part of a larger story that is shadowed by the author's doubts about how it should be told.

'He is wearing a dark suit, dark trousers and a light jacket, over a shirt and tie,' she writes about a photograph taken on a Sunday. If it had been during the week, she reasons, he would have been in his work overalls. She stands beside him in the photograph, holding the handlebars of her first bike. One foot is in the air, the other lightly touching the ground. Behind her is the open door of the cafe and an arrangement of flowers on the windowsill. 'It was customary to be photographed with your proudest possessions, in his case the business, the bicycle, and later the Citroën 4CV, on the roof of which he rests his hand, causing his jacket to ride up around his shoulders.' The bike, the car, the shop, even the flowers: these details index a social world made up of outlooks, habits, resentments, ways of dressing and presenting oneself, in short, an array of practices that each person imbibes. At what point, her book asks, did this array become visible as an array? When did it become something that could be viewed from a distance? What aspects have fallen to Ernaux to preserve?

'The testament, telling the heir what will rightfully be his, wills past possessions for a future,' writes Hannah Arendt. 'Without testament ... which selects and names, which hands down and preserves, which indicates where the treasures are and what their worth is—there seems to be no willed continuity in time and hence, humanly speaking, neither past nor future, only sempiternal change of the world and the biological cycle of living creatures in it.' Ernaux's writings push against this failure of testament. This does not involve the recuperation of the people and places that she left behind. Rather it involves giving voice to those elements that continue to press their claims on the present. 'I would ... like to capture the real woman,' she declares at the start of her book about her mother's life, *A Woman's Story*. 'The one who existed independently from me, born on the outskirts of a small Normandy town, and who died in the geriatric ward of a hospital in the suburbs of Paris.' She reflects on the type of book that might do justice to her life—one that contains elements of sociology, family history and fiction, literary in nature but also 'a cut below literature'. This qualification points to an unease that preoccupies the author. Writing grants her the pleasure of re-experiencing aspects of her life with her mother. It also forces her to confront the overwhelming reality of her death.

That writing both singles out and erases the specificity of a person's life is most forcefully expressed in a collection of diary entries and notes written by Ernaux during the period when her mother was in a nursing home suffering from late-stage dementia. Shunning any sense of objectivity or desire to stand apart from the events described, *I Remain in Darkness* is both witness to and directly implicated in the horror of her mother's decline. Yet such is the nature of the maternal bond that, in recording her mother's physical and mental dissolution, the book foretells the author's own decline. 'Saturday, threw up her coffee,' begins one entry. 'She was lying in bed, motionless. Her eyes were sunken, and red around the edges. I undressed her to change her clothes. Her body is white and flaccid. I started to sob. Because of time passing, because of the past. And because the body which I see is also mine.'

Embedded in this moving description of her mother's final days is a form of light that conjoins two bodies that share not only a common past but also a common fate. The daughter who looks after her ailing mother enfolds her life in the life of an other. Here responsibility manifest at the level of the body—its needs, its failings and encroaching darkness—and at the level of writing. 'She preferred giving to everybody, rather than taking from them,' Ernaux recalls about her mother. 'Isn't writing also a way of giving?' Framed in these terms, the goal of writing is to ensure that the processes of obliteration that determine the movement from one generation to the next do not preclude the possibility of continuity. In Ernaux's books this struggle is waged across two fronts: with feelings of out-of-placeness, humiliation and betrayal that, as a requirement of her elevation on the social scale, were suppressed, and with writing. This is what troubles and drives Ernaux's engagement with her past. It ensures that the testament provided remains provisional, alert to its limits and oversights, and, like the past it seeks to render, is always still-to-come.

IV

The light that passes between past and present marks the approach of people, places and things that the author can recognise and name, as well as experiences and feelings that register as a profound disquiet. In the closing sections of *The Years* this disquiet merges with the question of how to start a project that carries with it the guilt of being too long deferred. 'How to make the fresco of forty-five years coincide with the search for a self outside of History, the self of suspended moments transformed into the poems she wrote at twenty ("Solitude," etc.)?' One way to do this is through 'the palimpsest sensation'. Her point of reference is the state of half-sleep that follows sex with her much younger lover. 'She feels herself in several different moments of her life that float on top of each other. Time of an unknown nature takes hold of her consciousness and her body too. It is a time in which past and present overlap, without bleeding into each other, and where, it seems, she flickers in and out of all the shapes of being she has been.' This sensation brings with it the pleasure of slipping free of time's unrelenting forward movement. The downside is the elimination of everything that gives her existence its particularity. 'She wants to save her *circumstance*. And is the sensation itself not a product of history, of such great changes in the lives of women and men that one can feel it at the age of nearly fifty-eight, lying beside a man of twenty-nine, with no sense of wrong-doing, or indeed of pride?' The palimpsest sensation is thus an experience of different times lived simultaneously and the foretelling of what it means to lose one's time.

Ernaux's retirement from her job as a teacher coincides with two events that echo her future absence: the discovery of a tumour in her breast and the news that her eldest son's partner is pregnant. 'The ultrasound revealed a girl, and meanwhile she'd lost all her hair as a result of chemotherapy.' Burying a beloved cat in the backyard, she feels as if she is burying all the people she has lost—parents, relatives, a former lover, even that part of herself that was constantly changing, adopting new positions, attitudes, tastes. To her consternation, she has become 'immutable in a world that moves ahead in leaps and bounds.' Alongside this discovery is a more profound reorientation. Noting the distance between the type of life lived by her parents and the life that she has made for herself, she nonetheless feels herself drawing closer to them. 'As the time ahead objectively decreases, the time behind stretches farther and farther back, to long before birth and ahead to a time after her death. She imagines people saying, perhaps in thirty or forty years, that she was alive for the Algerian War, just as they used to say of her great-grandparents, "they were alive for the War of 1870."' This accentuates the urgency of her search for a form of writing that can accommodate her lived experience within its rendition of collective history.

The only way to achieve this, she concludes, is by immersing herself in images from her memory. In these closing sections, Ernaux places her bets on the capacity of images to bring together and synthesise not only past and present, but also individual and collective experience. 'All we have is our history, and it does not belong to us,' writes José Ortega y Gasset in the book's epigraph. Ernaux's memoir invites the reformulation: All we have are our images, and they do not belong to us. They do not belong to us because, for all the feelings of intimacy that images evoke, they also mark what reaches us from outside. They do not belong to us because they straddle the cleft between inside and outside. They do not belong to us because it is from their illumination that we garner a sense of not only our histories, relationships and passions, but also what the world looks like *without us*. For Ernaux, the image is where our future absence confronts us as a series of projections suspended just far enough in front of us to allow us an element of control, even a degree of pleasure. This is not a fading of light, merely a recognition that by binding her project so closely to the image's powerful illumination she becomes complicit in the disappearance of what she seeks to preserve. The clarity that images provide is, as she puts it near the start of the book, a 'twilight clarity'.

Perhaps it's not surprising, then, that in the book's closing pages she is reminded of her ambition as a young writer to 'find an unknown language that would unveil mysterious things, in the way of a clairvoyant'. In the memoir, the work of clairvoyance has turned its back on the future, in order to fix more firmly on images from the past. 'Now, more than anything, she would like to capture the light that suffuses faces that can no longer be seen and tables groaning with vanished food, the light that was already present in the stories of Sundays in childhood and has continued to settle upon things from the moment they are lived, a light from before.' A village fete, a hotel room, the wine tap at the Carrefour, a line of poetry, a merry-go-round at a park, the image of a young woman wearing a red coat, a film of little note, a half-torn poster on a wall, the gaze of a beloved cat at the moment of being euthanised ... In *The Years* these images drawn from memory constitute the history of a woman whose experiences are passing into *writing*. A final question presents itself: Is this something being restored—a type of powerful afterimage seared into the author's memory and projected onto the page? Or is it something experienced for the first time? A light from before whose wellspring is the struggle to write? By constantly circling back to these questions, Ernaux frames the book's status as something *to be written*.

In the book's finale, the sense of possibility associated with the time ahead has disappeared; age has left her feeling fixed in place, yet drawing ever closer to her forebears. But even so, the future continues to surge forth in the author's reflections on the urgency of the book that is still to be written, a book about the complicities that bind us to images. Of the finished book in front of us, its concluding line serves as testament—for all that has passed, as well as the struggle ahead: 'To save something from the time where we will never be again.'

9
As If It Were for the Last Time

I

In a million years,
when no one will be around any more
to even remember us faintly,
some of these places will.
Places have memories.
They remember everything.
It's engraved in stone.
It's deeper than the deepest waters.
Their memories are like sand dunes,
wandering on and on.

I guess that's why I take pictures of places:
I don't want to take them for granted.
I want to urge them
not to forget us.

Wim Wenders, 'Places', Pictures from the Surface of the Earth

In Wim Wenders's photographs, the camera is an instrument not simply for seeing but also for recording different gradations of time. During a visit to the Toshodaiji Temple in Nara, Japan, the photographer's attention is caught by a mound of moss growing at the foot of the temple wall. The forces of time and weather that gave birth to the moss have covered a section of the adjacent wall with a golden-brown patina that competes with the moss for ownership of the wall's surface. Another photograph taken during the visit to Nara shows a cross-section of a large rock. The countless fine lines and indentations that decorate the rock's surface also testify to the forces of weather, this time over a period not of years or decades but of centuries. A third image from the same trip recalibrates our sense of time yet again. It shows a tiny praying mantis perched near the edge of a void. In contrast to the vast expanse of time inscribed on the rock's surface, the image of the magnificent insect suggests a parcel of lived time that barely registers.

Inside the Toshodaiji Temple, Nara, Japan,
2000 © Wim Wenders

Rock with Inscriptions, Nara, Japan, 2000 © Wim Wenders

Praying Mantis, Nara, Japan, 2000 © Wim Wenders

Wenders's concern with using photography to document the passage of time can be traced to an earlier set of images taken during the preparation for his 1984 film, *Paris, Texas*. In an interview with the French critic Alain Bergala, he recounts how the experience of taking these photographs helped to familiarise him with the light and landscape of the American West. During the months he spent crisscrossing the country, he found himself drawn to particular types of surfaces: billboards, cinema facades and abandoned shopfronts worn away by the elements. These weathered surfaces clarified photography's documentary nature. 'The way I see it,' he tells Bergala, 'it's a vital part of photography, seeing something and recording it as if it were the last possible chance to do so. To my mind, that's the "end of the world" side of photography.' During the same discussion he acknowledges the other side of this sensibility: once taken, the photograph serves to perpetuate the existence of things even after their extinction.

To look at something as if it were for the last time, as if the thing being looked at were in the process of disappearing. For Wenders, photography has a number of overlapping functions: it is a medium with its own aesthetic requirements and demands; a way of reflecting on the nature of cinema; and, most challenging of all, a form of thinking in which we confront the ending and surviving of things.

II

In the interview with Bergala, Wenders recalls a piece of advice the American director Nicholas Ray gave to his actors: 'Even if you're only asking for a light, even if you're only saying good day, you have to do it as if you thought it could be the last time.' We know that the action performed by the screen actor can be repeated again and again. But what Ray's statement alludes to is that the moment in which the action is performed can never be repeated. Uniquely among the arts, film and photography preserve this unrepeatable moment. 'All films are ultimately documentaries,' Wenders extrapolates, 'because in passing, unintentionally, they record the clouds crossing the sky or a flock of birds somewhere in the background or someone walking by who doesn't notice he's being filmed.'

In an appreciation of Ray's 1952 film *The Lusty Men*, he reaffirms this view of film's documentary qualities. He recounts how Ray began the shoot with a script of just twenty-six pages. Each night, Ray worked with his screenwriters and actors to prepare material for the next day's shooting. The outcome of this method is exemplified by a sequence near the start of the film that begins with a lone figure (Robert Mitchum) hobbling through an empty rodeo arena. The sound of the wind blowing across the arena counterpoints the hoopla of the earlier scenes of the rodeo riders. Arriving at a dilapidated farmhouse and finding the front door locked, he walks around to the back and retrieves from under the house an old rodeo program, a six-shooter pistol without handle grips and a small tobacco tin. The unhurried manner in which these activities unfold opens the door for a relationship to the film in which the documentary status of the images assumes equal weight to the fiction: 'Without any pressure, without any sense of haste, every shot gradually becomes a sign in some sort of runic script, that you slowly see and hear. A song. Mitchum's slightly limping gait. A landscape opening up. Trees standing alone. A wavy line of soft hills on the horizon. A remote farmhouse without even a path leading up to it. The short shadows of the midday sun.'

In Wenders's description of the film's opening moments, it is not just a character that we see, but also the actor, Robert Mitchum. It is not just a location that we remember, but also the geography of an actual place. Overall, it is not just a story that we recall, but also an event whose existence, captured by the camera, is projected on the screen. This insistence on the film's eventness lies at the heart of the photographic attitude that pervades Wenders's films.

We can trace its impact by turning to another occasion when he pays tribute to Ray. Made in 1976, *Kings of the Road* (*Im Lauf der Zeit*) deals with the encounter between Bruno Winter (Rüdiger Vogler), who makes his living travelling across the eastern regions of West Germany in a converted bus, repairing and servicing film projectors, and Robert Lander (Hanns Zischler), whose background, marital status and occupation remain, for most of the film's first hour, undisclosed. That Robert is fleeing a crisis in his home life is indicated by his action of tearing up a postcard-sized photograph of a house, while speeding along a country road in his VW Beetle. As Bruno watches Robert drive his car headlong into a river, it's obvious that both characters have reached the end of the road. The time they spend together, driving from one town or village to the next, does not generate a new direction for either character. Rather, it results in something more fleeting: a sense that time spent with another person can be a source of connection as well as conflict, and that returning to the places that constitute our past can bring with it comfort as well as grief.

The film's most overt tribute to Ray occurs when Wenders replays the scene of Mitchum's return to his former home. But whereas the homecoming in *The Lusty Men* takes only a few moments, Bruno's return to his childhood home, first by motorcycle with sidecar and then by rowboat, is in keeping with the film's digressive approach. Even when he arrives, the drama is slow to emerge. As we watch the character take stock of the abandoned house, it's unclear what types of emotions are being stirred. That powerful emotions have indeed been triggered is evidenced by Bruno throwing a heavy object through one of the windows. No explanation is given for this; neither are we told the reason for the tears that he wipes from his face later that night. By withholding these explanations, Wenders ensures that the focus of the drama extends beyond character psychology to incorporate other scenic elements, such as the space in which the actor moves, the material objects in that space, and the actor's gestures perceived as gestures rather than simply external manifestations of an inner life. Underpinning all this is his insistence on keeping two ways of treating the cinematic image alive: on the one hand, as part of the telling of a story and, on the other, as the record of a particular time. Across Wenders's films, this approach gives birth to stories in which narrative and character development are prone to suspension—stories in which nothing seems to happen, except the passing of time.

Near the end of *Kings of the Road*, Bruno reflects on the journey to his home. 'I'm glad we went to the Rhine,' he tells Robert. 'For the first time I see myself as someone who has gone through a certain time, and this time is my history. The feeling is quite comforting.' Rather than some childhood trauma, the thing that Bruno confronts in the house is time. The abandoned rooms embody a parcel of time that is over and cannot be revivified. He calls this encounter comforting, but his actions suggest that, at a deeper level, it is also disturbing. This disturbance lends weight to the conclusion that Bruno confronts in the house the same thing that Wenders confronts in his written reflections on *The Lusty Men*: a sense of time specific to cinema. Bruno's homecoming affirms a view of cinema as a type of memento mori. Remember this, Wenders insists. Remember both the film from which Bruno's actions are taken and the cinema's capacity to give us an image of time that sweeps away all traces of human life. For Wenders, the places and events that we remember and manage to return to through the cinema have the capacity to reciprocate this investment. They do so by speaking to us of our own passing.

III

To look at something as if it were for the last time, as if the thing being looked at were in the process of disappearing. Tracing the history of this attitude leads to the films of Ray. Pursuing a different course, we arrive at another figure central to the photographic attitude informing Wenders's work: the American photographer Walker Evans. 'The photos Walker Evans took in the Depression,' Wenders proposes in the interview with Bergala, 'were just that: preserving something that was going to disappear in three or four years' time, in your eye and in your memory.' The affinity between Wenders and Evans is evident in their fascination with images of ruin and decay. In 1935, Evans accepted a commission from the New York industrialist Gifford Cochran to document surviving examples of Greek Revival-style architecture in the South. The photographs were intended as illustrations for a book on the architecture of the South that never made it to print. Despite their concern with the remnants of a once grand lifestyle, the dominant tone of the images is not nostalgia but rather a disquieting sense of time's passing. The dilapidation that marks the structures photographed by Evans indexes a movement of time that is unstoppable. Looking at these images, we register what it means for people and things to get old, to lose their sheen.

Room in Louisiana Plantation House, Walker Evans, March 1935. The Metropolitan Museum of Art, Gilman Collection, Purchase, Ann Tenenbaum and Thomas H. Lee Gift, 2005 (2005.100.322) © Walker Evans Archive, The Metropolitan Museum of Art.

The depredations that accompany the passing of time are evident in a photograph taken during a visit to the Belle Grove Plantation in White Castle, Louisiana. The details on the Corinthian columns that stand at the entrance to the abandoned room evidence the level of care and expense that went into the room's construction. At the same time, the watermarks, exposed woodwork and crumbling plaster are sure signs of impending dilapidation. 'It is only a matter of time before the inside becomes the outside,' Geoff Dyer observes about the room's fate. 'The ceiling will be first to go, followed, eventually, by the doors, then the walls. The Corinthian columns and pilasters—which one associates with the open-air ruins of classical antiquity—make the room seem predisposed to such an eventuality. As things stand, though, the room is still managing to hold its own: to enclose time within its walls (as Evans encloses it within the picture frame) and keep it at bay.'

The power of Evans's photograph resides in the coexistence of this accretion of decay with the fading signs of a grand past. Writing in the third person, the photographer provides his own summation of its significance: 'Evans was, and is, interested in what any present time will look like as the past.' This concern with evoking different registers of time is not restricted to his photographs of formerly grand estates. It is also evident in his images of places with no such pretensions. One of his most well-known photographs from the 1930s shows the interior of a Black barbershop in Atlanta. Although the shop is empty, the towels draped across the arms and headrests of the chairs wait in readiness for the next person to walk through the door. The towels, the worn leather chairs, the lanterns lined up on a shelf, the hat resting on the bureau: these things wait for us. But they also speak of a life that happens without us, a life that happens after we have left—or are yet to arrive. These objects are, in other words, emblems of photography itself. They affirm the medium's capacity to induce what the film scholar Miriam Bratu Hansen eloquently describes as 'an awareness of a history that does not include us'.

Barber Shop Interior, Atlanta, Georgia, Walker Evans, March 1936. The Metropolitan Museum of Art, Walker Evans Archive, 1994 (1994.258.353) © Walker Evans Archive, The Metropolitan Museum of Art.

In his prose poem 'Places', Wenders explains why he takes pictures of places: 'I don't want to take them for granted. / I want to urge them / not to forget us.' Urging places 'not to forget us' is not about personification. Rather, it involves a type of inversion whereby human existence is looked at from the point of view of a material realm that does not include us. The histories evident in these places are histories in eclipse. This is the photographic vantage point that underpins the work of Wenders and Evans. The question we have yet to respond to is: how does Wenders deal with the dilemma of coming *after* Evans? That when he looks at a billboard, a shop front, a road sign in the American West he is also looking at a photograph by Evans of a billboard, a shop front, a road sign in the American West? 'There can be no after without a debt, an unsettled relation, a haunting,' writes the scholar Gerhard Richter. Our question then becomes: how does this 'unsettled relation' leave its mark on Wenders's images?

IV

In 2001, Wenders spent a week in the coastal town that serves as one of the principal settings in Yasujirô Ozu's masterpiece *Tokyo Story* (1953). The photo-book that documents the visit frames the dilemma of coming after as a matter of seeing things that one already has in mind:

> Onomichi showed me once again
> that we don't just 'see.'
> We recognize what we already 'have in mind.'
> We have learned to appreciate certain things,
> want to see them all over again
> and in the process disregard others.
> We find (so often) the very thing we were looking for.

This is another aspect of the photographic attitude pervading Wenders's work. His awareness of recognising things already 'in mind' positions the films and photographs as part of a continuum of approaches, and carries with it certain obligations. 'To make films is for Wenders in a sense to watch once more and remember the films one had already seen,' the film scholar Thomas Elsaesser explains. 'Action could only be the retelling of action. The point was not to film something that had never been shown before but to show something in such a way that it appeared to be a memory of something one had already seen.' Taking up this suggestion, we can say that, for Wenders, taking photographs is not a matter of photographing something that has never been shown before, but of capturing something so that it appears as a memory of something already seen. In his photographs, memory and the effects of time passing operate side by side. Walter Benjamin outlines a similar interaction in his essay on Proust, describing the author's true interest as 'the passage of time in its most real—that is, space-bound—form, and this passage nowhere holds sway more openly than in remembrance within and aging without.' Benjamin's summation crystallises a question that is as important to Wenders's photographs as it is to the design of Proust's monumental work of literature: how to remember well? How to mark both the disappearance and the living-on of what has come before? These questions inform the dilemma of coming after.

One way Wenders responds to this dilemma is through writing. In *Journey to Onomichi*, for example, his written text emphasises the impossibility of separating his vision of Japan from the vision of others:

> The Japan I perceive through my camera
> is strictly my very own sight.
> (Or 'insight'?)
> It is shaped by the history of Japanese Cinema,
> (that I got to know in Paris and New York,
> long before I ever set foot in Japan for the first time,)
> but also by Caspar David Friedrich, Vermeer, and Hopper,
> by Walker Evans, Sebastiao Salgado and Joel Meyerowitz,
> by Van Morrison, Dylan and Lou Reed,
> by Peter Handke, Walker Percy and Bruce Chatwin
> by my wife's black and white photography
> and by everything else I ever saw, read, heard and loved.

This recitation of names places Ozu's influence in the context of other influences that have shaped Wenders's photographic approach. At the same time, it serves another purpose that is also directly related to the recognition of coming after. 'My stories always start from images,' Wenders wrote in 1982. 'My stories always begin with places, cities and landscapes or roads.' Through their integration of image and text, Wenders's photo-books represent a continuation of these principles. The stories they tell are dispersed across a vast range of places: Cuba, Australia, the United States, Japan, Russia and Israel. But each story is grounded in a single defining experience, the experience of arriving at a place one has never been to before and finding in that place traces of a story that has already been told. Even before we take our first step, memory arrives in advance, populating the world with everything we have seen or heard. The image is a record of these moments of displacement and recognition.

Framed as an account of his time in Onomichi, Wenders's written text documents how the discovery of what one already has in mind coincides with the experience of something new. Walking through the city's streets, he struggles to master the basic requirements: 'I buy unidentifiable refreshments from vending machines. / At a fast food stand I point at dishes / for which I have no name. / In the streetcar or bus I hold out / my handful of coins to the driver.' Gradually, he comes to understand this unfamiliar place through his memory of Ozu's film:

> It was all there:
> The coastal waters with the nearby offshore islands,
> (one could take this for the mouth of a big river,)
> the flat houses, built against the hills,
> the temples nestling among tall trees in vast parks,
> and most of all: the railroad line
> winding its way down along the coast.
> (The trains play a big part in the film ...)

Even though Onomichi had become unrecognisable from the city depicted in Ozu's film, just enough remains for Wenders to catch sight of 'the old days' of Onomichi. Rounding a corner, he asks himself: 'Those men casting their lines on the quay walls / and the smoking onlookers around them, / didn't I see them in black and white?' This is what it means to tell stories from the point of view of images: to wander through a world that is unfamiliar, yet also inhabited by the phantoms of stories and figures that have come before. The written account of Wenders's journey to Onomichi affirms that coming after is not merely about seeing what one already has in mind. It is also about the struggle to understand how this continuation unsettles our experience of the present. The same can be said of his attachment to photography and film more generally. Both media align our existence with the existence of things that have passed and imbue these things with an afterlife that calls us to account as temporal beings.

'This is how it is. Nothing else, says the picture of the empty red bench in front of the camouflage colors of a large warship. Nowhere the hint of an affect, the mirroring of a strange aesthetic. No afterimage of the picture. No connotations. Nameless.' In a short accompanying essay, Heiner Bastian claims that Wenders's images of Onomichi mirror Ozu's refusal to aggrandise the details of the material world. On one level, this is true. But it does not rule out the suggestion of other figures and influences positioned just over the photographer's shoulder. *The Sofa* shows a tatty grey sofa pushed up against the wall of a restaurant. Although nobody is sitting on it, the signs of wear and

The Sofa, Onomichi, Japan, 2005 © Wim Wenders

tear testify to years of occupancy. Nobody is sitting on the sofa, but soon somebody will be. Like the chairs in Evans's photo of the Black barbershop in Atlanta, it waits for us; perhaps it even waits for Evans, or his memory at least, to find its way back to this unfamiliar city located between the past and the present.

IV

To look at something as if it were for the last time, as if the thing being looked at were in the process of disappearing. We now know that this involves acknowledging the figures who have brought us to where we are and speak to us of what lies ahead. In *Journey to Onomichi* this occurs through a combination of still images and written text. Wenders's films have other resources at their disposal. Slowing things down, allowing the narrative to digress and ensuring that place is as important as character: this is how Wenders draws out the implications of Ray's legacy for his own approach to cinema. Just as significant is his employment of gesture. Again, I am thinking of Bruno in *Kings of the Road* throwing the heavy object through the window of his former home. Up to this point, everything about the homecoming had been about the past: Bruno's slow movement through the rooms, the dust and debris covering the remaining pieces of furniture, the dim light filtering through the windows. Smashing the window serves to 'change the beat': its violence demands a new set of responses from the actor and the audience. Acting coaches employ these sudden changes to ensure that the process of performance does not solidify into a replaying of predetermined emotions and meanings. This does not prevent the actor from using skills learnt through training, habit and memory. But it does ensure that these things do not hinder what Lee Strasberg and others refer to as 'the illusion of the first time'.

In an unpublished fragment, Walter Benjamin describes Charlie Chaplin's capacity to integrate his gestures with the discontinuous nature of filmic movement. 'Each single movement he makes is composed of a succession of staccato bits of movement. Whether it is his walk, the way he handles his cane, or the way he raises his hat—always the same jerky sequence of tiny movements applies the law of the cinematic image sequence to human motorial functions.' Chaplin's jerky movements suggest both the interpenetration of the performer's physiological impulses with the machinery of cinema, and a playing with the structures and rhythms that are part of everyday life. Jumping forward nearly four decades, Bruno's unexpected smashing of the window represents another instance in which an actor's physical actions alert us to the discontinuities that determine the camera's engagement with the world. At the heart of this process is a twofold event in which movement is, for a split second, interrupted and set differently.

In photography, the effects of this interruption are held fast for our contemplation. In film, the unfolding of images tends to fabricate an experience that is seamless. But it doesn't take much for the originating disturbance to surge back to life: a sudden look or gesture on the part of the actor that disrupts the confines of character, an element of decor or setting that exceeds its scenic requirements, a moment of immobility when the unfolding of images appears to stall. Regardless of how it occurs, the outcome is a re-engagement with the fraction of a second during which an action or event is interrupted by the camera and set differently. In *Kings of the Road* Bruno's violent gesture is geared to the accomplishment of this outcome. Its disruption of the scene allows us to pinpoint how the re-engagement with the past coincides with the emergence of something new. It also ensures that the dilemma of coming after is not just about comprehending the legacy of the past but also about creating the possibility of a future.

We can now add nuance our understanding of Nicholas Ray's advice to his actors about performing each action as if it were for the last time. To see or do something as if it were for the last time: finally, we can see that, for Wenders, this is synonymous with seeing or doing something as if it were for the first time. The astonishing thing about film and photography is that everything we see has happened for the first and last time.

10
The Work of Mourning

I

Georgia Metaxas, *Untitled #12*, from the series *The Mourners*, 2010–11

'Mourning is regularly the reaction to the loss of a loved person, or to the loss of some abstraction which has taken the place of one,' Freud tells us. These abstractions can include one's country or a deeply held ideal. His central point is that mourning is not pathological. Its primary purpose is to enable the mourner to accommodate the loss of the person or thing being mourned. He refers to this as a process of 'reality testing' in which, bit by bit, the libido detaches itself from the loved object. 'It is a matter of general observation that people never willingly abandon a libidinal position,' he concedes. 'This opposition can be so intense that a turning away from reality takes place and a clinging to the object through the medium of a hallucinatory wishful psychosis. Normally, respect for reality gains the day. Nevertheless its orders cannot be obeyed at once.' This concession brings to the surface a question that complicates Freud's insistence on mourning's utilitarian dimensions: How long to mourn? What constitutes its proper duration? Raising this question grounds the activity of mourning more firmly in the context of its social functioning: in other words, in how it connects us to and separates us from others.

II

That mourning is not a phase we pass through but an experience that persists is central to Roland Barthes's *Mourning Diary*. Written in the weeks and months after his mother's death, and published after his own death at the age of 64, less than three years after his mother's passing, these diary entries—sometimes just a few words; more often, a couple of sentences—underline mourning's resistance to chronology. 'There is a time when death is an *event*, an ad-venture, and as such mobilizes, interests, activates, tetanizes,' he observes in an entry dated 15 November. 'And then one day it is no longer an event, it is another *duration*, compressed, insignificant, not narrated, grim, without recourse: true mourning not susceptible to any narrative dialectic.' Two weeks later, he describes his experience of mourning as undiminished, 'not subject to erosion, to time. Chaotic, erratic: *moments* (of distress, of love of life) as *fresh* now as on the first day.' Such is the acuteness of this feeling that it shuts down the one thing that might ascribe meaning to his loss. 'Depression comes when, in the depths of despair, I cannot save myself by my attachment to writing.' And elsewhere: 'Less and less to write, to say, except this (which I can tell no one).'

For someone whose attachment to writing has always been central to the tensions and competing forces that constitute his subjectivity—a means to give these tensions and competing forces form—this is unthinkable. But this is what his mother's nonexistence forces him to confront: that which resists thinking. 'Now, from time to time, there unexpectedly rises within me, like a bursting bubble: the realization that *she no longer exists, she no longer exists*, totally and forever. This is a flat condition, utterly unadjectival—dizzying because *meaningless* (without any possible interpretation).' The mourning diary maps the reverberations of this dreadful realisation.

Biographers tell us that Barthes spent the short time between his mother's death and his own completing a number of seminal publications, preparing and teaching new courses at the Collège de France, compiling research notes for future projects, and accepting invitations from international universities to talk about his work. By any measure, a time when he is immersed in the world and yet also, by his own account, turned away from it.

III

Comprising thirteen photographic portraits of elderly women dressed in black and positioned in front of a black velvet screen, Georgia Metaxas's *The Mourners* also considers how mourning connects us to and separates us from others. In the photographs, the black backdrop works with the black clothing to reinforce the sense of a common experience. So too does the manner in which the women have turned their bodies and expressions away from the camera. But the more we look at these images, the more these common elements draw attention

First row, left to right: *Untitled #11, Untitled #20, Untitled #2*, from the series *The Mourners*, 2010–11
Second row: *Untitled #28, Untitled #7, Untitled #1*, from the series *The Mourners*, 2010–11
Third row: *Untitled #16, Untitled #27, Untitled #21*, from the series *The Mourners*, 2010–11
Fourth row: *Untitled #25, Untitled #6, Untitled #17*, from the series *The Mourners*, 2010–11

to markers of difference. For example, six of the women wear traditional Orthodox headscarves. If we look closely, we can see that draped on the chests of five are necklaces displaying various religious icons and crucifixes. If we look closer still, we realise that, in one case, the item dangling from the necklace is not an icon or crucifix but a small black-and-white photograph of the face of a man that has been embossed onto a gold plate.

These differences alert us to the challenge underpinning the photographer's project. Any rendition of the state of being that we refer to as mourning must acknowledge two seemingly opposing starting points: the universal nature of the experience in question, and the singularity of both the mourner and the life being mourned. 'Stripped back to the point where only the faintest trace of the sitter's surroundings remain,' Metaxas observes in an artist's statement, 'the portrait brings the viewer to the periphery of an ultimately private space.' How do the photographs embed this ultimately private space within a space of communal engagement?

Describing the influences that shape her work, Metaxas refers to a tradition of documentary photography that focuses on everyday rituals. Her most sustained engagement with this tradition is the series of photographs that document the religious celebrations and cultural life of Melbourne's Greek community. Spanning the late 1990s and early 2000s, when the photographer was still in her twenties, these photographs fulfil the desire of the community's members to be seen as a community, united by a shared ethnicity and history, while also counteracting the tendency to render this community monolithic. The experience of community life on show in the photographs occurs in the context of an encounter—on the part of the photographer and the viewer—with the singularities of the people that make up this life: a dancer backstage, taking a moment to adjust her scarf while her friends carry on with their chatter; an altar boy holding open the door through which the photographer is passing; the pain on a Cypriot woman's face as she holds in front of her a framed photograph of missing loved ones.

Georgia Metaxas, *Image #2*, from the series *Greek Easter*, 2000

Georgia Metaxas, *Image #3*, from the series *Cyprus March*, 2000

In the introduction to a collection of photographs of the faces of New York subway commuters captured by Walker Evans using a 35mm camera hidden in his coat pocket, James Agee identifies both a vast gallery of social types and the imprints of a unique life: 'Each carries in the postures of his body, in his hands, in his face, in the eyes, the signatures of a time and place in the world.' Something similar can be said of the faces and bodies in Metaxas's work. In her photographs of Greek Easter celebrations, we are drawn to the ornateness of the priests' robes, the beauty of the bier held aloft by a sea of worshippers, as well as the vibrancy of the flowers decorating the church. But just as insistent are the mortal bodies at the heart of the event: the grey-haired woman kissing the Bible held up by the priest; the old folk sitting around a tree, resting their legs; the three women standing during the ceremony while those around them are seated. In these photographs, the individuals that constitute the community take on a collective face; at the same time, they are revealed to be subject to those forces that mark the coming into being and passing away of each life.

Georgia Metaxas, *Image #6*, from the series *Greek Easter*, 2000

This revelation shifts our understanding of a community's foundation away from a shared ethnicity or race to something that implicates us in the other's fate. To put this more directly, the darkness that surrounds the members of the congregation in the Greek Easter photographs is more than a stylistic effect. It exposes the faces and bodies on show to the limits of what can be perceived. '*Community itself, in sum, is nothing but this exposition,*' writes the philosopher Jean-Luc Nancy. 'It is the community of finite beings, and as such it is itself a *finite* community.' In Metaxas's photographs, this is what binds the members of the community—what they have in common: their shared finitude.

IV

This rendition of community links Metaxas's earlier photographs to the images in *The Mourners*. The photographer drew her subjects from Melbourne's Greek, Maltese, Italian, Spanish and Lebanese communities. To create the photographs, she assembled a portable studio comprising a black backdrop, a tripod, a medium-format Mamiya film camera, a single modified light and foam reflector, carefully arranged to capture highlights and shadow details, and a stool on which the subjects were seated. The studio was set up in kitchens, living rooms, church halls, nursing homes—wherever the subjects felt most comfortable. In selecting which of the women to photograph, she asked each a series of questions: For whom are you wearing black? Do you wear it every day? How long have you been wearing it? The most important question was the last: Will you wear it for the rest of your life? This question implies a relationship to mourning that is not a phase or duty, but a fundamental change in one's relationship to the world. Moreover, it establishes the terms of a communality that is principled on what is common to all.

Where *The Mourners* differs from the photographer's earlier work is that it draws not on the documentary tropes that characterised the images of the Greek community, but on an older set of photographic and art-historical traditions. Perhaps the most obvious of these is associated with the early photographic portraitists such as David Octavius Hill and Julia Margaret Cameron, whose work relied on the sitter remaining perfectly still to accommodate the long exposure times of the first cameras. Walter Benjamin claims that this caused the subject of the photograph 'to focus his entire life in the moment rather than hurrying on past it; during the considerable period of the exposure, the subject (as it were) grew into the picture'. In Metaxas's photographs too, the arrangement of the figures in front of the camera suggests a type of temporal compression. The black materials and lighting capture the details of each of the faces. Each line, each furrow speaks of an experience etched deeply in the life history of the sitter, one that binds the women and indexes their separateness.

Metaxas's other point of reference is a tradition of absorptive painting that reached its high point around the middle of the eighteenth century, and counted as its exponents such painters as Jean-Baptiste-Siméon Chardin, Jean-Baptiste Greuze and, later, Jacques-Louis David. This tradition developed in reaction to the decorative artifice of the rococo that held sway in the early part of the century. The primary spokesperson for this tradition was Denis Diderot. In his *Essais sur la peinture*, Diderot argues that figures in a painting must give the impression of taking no notice of the beholder. He provides this warning to painters: 'If you lose your feeling for the difference between the man who presents himself in society and the man engaged in an action, between the man who is alone and the man who is looked at, throw your brushes into the fire. You will academicize all your figures, you will make them still and unnatural.' 'What this meant in practice,' the art historian Michael Fried explains, 'was that the represented figures had to be made to appear entirely engrossed or ... *absorbed* in their actions, feelings, and states of mind; figures so absorbed were felt to be oblivious to everything but the objects of their attention, including, especially, the beholder standing before the canvas.' Artists who failed to achieve this state were seen by Diderot to have lapsed into a reliance on postures and attitudes solely intended to impress the viewer. Instead of affecting absorption, the figures in a painting would be guilty of that most reviled of painterly sins: theatricality.

To help painters maintain the fiction, Diderot formulated a conception of painting in which the representation of action conformed to principles of pictorial unity derived from classical drama. The epitome of such a form of dramatic representation was the tableau whose point of view, self-sufficiency and instantaneousness were seen as the best way for the artist to arrest the attention of the beholder and hold them in front of the painting in a type of absorptive engagement that, paradoxically, effects their absence from the scene depicted. As Fried surmises: 'Only by establishing the fiction of [the beholder's] absence or non-existence could his actual placement before and enthrallment by the painting be secured.'

In *The Mourners* also, the action of turning the bodies and expressions of the women away from the camera works in concert with the rendition of absorptive states to secure our engagement in front of the photographs. This affinity situates Metaxas's images alongside those of other photographers. In the early work of Cindy Sherman and Jeff Wall, for example, absorptive motifs go hand in hand with an acknowledgement of the 'to-be-seenness' of the images. In Sherman's *Untitled Film Stills* this involves the photographer placing herself at the centre of a series of scenes that evoke the tradition of the Hollywood publicity still. This evocation of theatricality occurs at the same time as the poses adopted by the photographer direct her attention to somewhere other than where the viewer is located. In Wall's light-box photographs the employment of figures that pay no mind to the viewer's presence occurs concurrently with the rendering of a level of compositional detail that undercuts the everydayness of the actions on show. There is also the matter of the large size of the images that, as Fried notes, makes them purpose-built for viewing on a museum wall.

Regardless of the differences involved, the connection between Metaxas, Sherman and Wall hinges on the creation of a theatricality in which the negation of the viewer's presence occurs simultaneously with an acknowledgement of the picture's status as a picture. The outcome is a renewal of a centuries-old tradition, and the starting point for a reflection on the nature and purpose of photographic representation. How should a photograph engage with its viewer? How is this engagement best sustained? What attitudes are conducive to its accomplishment?

Printed just smaller than life-size, Metaxas's photographs do not have the grand scale of Wall's images. Also absent are the self-conscious melodramatic elements of Sherman's filmic reconstructions. Her connection to the absorptive tradition is more modest *and* more direct. The best way to parse this connection is to note that the theatricality that characterises her compositions has been divorced from the accomplishment of an action. Taking the place of action is something that challenges the very idea of a scene. 'The dying of Others is not something that we experience in an authentic sense,' writes Martin Heidegger. 'At most we are always just "there alongside."' Heidegger's proposition requires us to recast the photographer's arrangement of the bodies and expressions of her subjects as enacting not simply a *turning away* from the viewer, but also a *turning towards* something that binds the women to the person being mourned and designates the limits of this connection—something that catalyses and arrests our thinking.

To put this more forcefully, the carefully wrought luminosity that renders the faces and bodies of the mourners operates in connection with a surrounding darkness. This evokes the delicate relationship between light and darkness that determines the emergence of the photographic image. Too much light, and the image is lost. Too little, and it fails to appear. In *The Mourners* this nod to the conditions governing the image's visibility draws attention to that which cannot be made visible—a blind spot present in the grain and tone of the photographic print.

V

'Nothing to say about the death of one whom I love most, nothing to say about her photograph, which I contemplate without ever being able to get to the heart of it, to transform it,' Barthes agonises. 'The only "thought" I can have is that at the end of this first death, my own death is inscribed; between the two, nothing more than waiting.' This is also what the mourners do. They wait. And through this waiting they, like the subjects of the early photographic portraitists, grow into the picture. Their time coincides with the time of the photograph, a time in which we experience the transformation of a present moment into the past, in which the confirmation of life coincides with the affirmation of death. But we need to be careful: *The Mourners* does not affirm death. How could such a thing be affirmed? Rather, it gives expression to its immanence, its nearness-to-us. This is what draws us to the women. It makes their mourning not a private matter, but the basis of their relationship to others.

The question that keeps recurring is: can we extrapolate from the photographs a renewed understanding of community? The supposition underpinning these images is that by addressing ourselves to the delimiting power of death we can reformulate a community's foundations, away from a culture or ethnicity or language, possessed by some and not by others, to what is common. In this formulation, the recognition of the other's likeness occurs at the same time as an acknowledgement of their finitude. This is what gives the connections on which the community is founded their openness and life.

Drawing attention to these connections forefronts the photographer's own relationship to the women in the images. Metaxas is part of a generation whose histories overlapped with the histories of these women. If they were not part of her own family, they were present at the Easter celebrations or the funerals or mnimosina. Perhaps they appeared in the photo albums that were handed down by a parent or grandparent. Just as the earlier photographs of Melbourne's Greek community confirm the photographer's place in its rituals and celebrations (while allowing her to keep her distance), the photographs of the mourners facilitate a reconsideration of what binds her to this generation of women. The philosopher Maurice Blanchot writes of a form of friendship that is forged on our exposure to the possibility of the other's absence. 'It is in life itself that that absence of someone else has to be met. It is with that absence ... that friendship is brought into play and lost at each moment.' This elusive friendship that is always on the verge of disappearing is another way to consider the communal affiliations operating in Metaxas's photographs. Bound to an act of mourning that cannot be reduced to a matter of so many days or months or years, the mourners wait—not for something to happen, but for something that has already happened ... and is just up ahead.

The thought that persists is that, in documenting these women and paying tribute to their lives, Metaxas is undertaking her own work of mourning whose protocols and rituals coincide with the taking of the photograph. Having assembled her makeshift studio, carefully adjusted the lighting and positioned her subject on the stool, she stands behind the camera, looking down at the image captured in the glass viewfinder, waiting for just the right moment to press the shutter. She waits for them, knowing full well that they will wait for her. The mourners are embodiments of ways of being that have passed, anachronisms that we are surprised to find still exist, and figures of what is still to come in our experience of this world. They invite us to approach, and they keep their distance.

Cities and the Dead

I

'Never in all my travels had I ventured as far as Adelma,' recalls Marco Polo in Italo Calvino's *Invisible Cities*. 'It was dusk when I landed there. On the dock the sailor who caught the rope and tied it to the bollard resembled a man who had soldiered with me and was dead.' Walking through the bustling fish market, Polo catches sight of an old man hauling a basket of sea urchins. 'I thought I recognized him; when I turned, he had disappeared down an alley, but I realized that he looked like a fisherman who, already old when I was a child, could no longer be among the living.' A little further on, he encounters a man in the grip of fever: 'My father a few days before his death had yellow eyes and a growth of beard like this man. I turned my gaze aside; I no longer dared look anyone in the face.' And so it goes. Each encounter with the inhabitants of this city at the farthest point in his travels brings to mind figures from his past who are no longer among the living. He sees a girl standing on a balcony, holding a piece of string attached to a basket that has been lowered to an old woman selling vegetables on the street below. Her face appears identical to that of a girl in his home village who, in the throes of love, had killed herself. 'The vegetable vendor raised her face: she was my grandmother.'

The story of Adelma is one of five that appear under the theme 'Cities and the Dead'. Each one is about the relationships that bind the living to the dead. The distinctive thing about the story of Adelma is that it speaks directly of Polo's own circumstances. 'You reach a moment in life,' he tells himself about his encounters in the far-flung city, 'when, among the people you have known, the dead outnumber the living. And the mind refuses to accept more faces, more expressions: on every new face you encounter, it prints the old forms, for each one it finds the most suitable mask.' The story of Adelma, then, is also a story about arriving at an age when, by sheer weight of numbers, the dead claim priority over the living. *Middle age? Old age?* More important than the name we give to this age or the point in one's life when it occurs is the type of thinking it initiates. 'Perhaps, for each of them, I also resembled someone who was dead,' Polo speculates. 'I had barely arrived at Adelma and I was already one of them, I had gone over to their side, absorbed in that kaleidoscope of eyes, wrinkles, grimaces.'

II

In Polo's chronicles the closest equivalent to Adelma is Laudomia. Like every city, Laudomia is a double city. There is the Laudomia made up of the city's living inhabitants. There is also the Laudomia made up of the ever-swelling ranks of the dead. 'The more the Laudomia of the living becomes crowded and expanded, the more the expanse of tombs increases beyond the walls. The streets of the Laudomia of the dead are just wide enough to allow the gravedigger's cart to pass, and many windowless buildings look out on them; but the pattern of the streets and the arrangement of the dwellings repeat those of the living Laudomia, and in both, families are more and more crowded together, in compartments crammed one above the other.'

In Polo's account of the two Laudomias, it's not clear if the dead are the forebears of the living or the living themselves, at some future point. Better to say that they are both. This is why, when they pay their respects to the dead, the city's residents search for their own names on the cemetery's stone slabs. 'Like the city of the living, this other city communicates a history of toil, anger, illusions, emotions; only here all has become necessary, divorced from chance, categorized, set in order. And to feel sure of itself, the living Laudomia has to seek in the Laudomia of the dead the explanation of itself, even at the risk of finding more there, or less.'

The feelings of anxiety that accompany these endeavours are compounded by the presence of a third Laudomia, whose inhabitants are the unborn. The relationship between the living and the unborn is, like the relationship between the living and the dead, transactional: it is a means for the living to seek reassurance about their own lives and actions. But, here again, little comfort is obtained. 'One man is concerned with leaving behind him an illustrious reputation, another wants his shame to be forgotten; all would like to follow the thread of their own actions' consequences; but the more they sharpen their eyes, the less they can discern a continuous line; the future inhabitants of Laudomia seem like dots, grains of dust, detached from any before or after.' The feelings of alarm triggered by these engagements cluster around two ways of conceiving the expanse of time that lies in wait for each person. The first is the thought that the sheer scale of all those yet to be born will inevitably wipe away all trace of the living. The second is bound to the realisation that, at some point, the place known as Laudomia will disappear, 'and all its citizens with it; in other words the generations will follow one another until they reach a certain number and will then go no further'.

The story concludes with the image of an hourglass. 'Each passage between birth and death is a grain of sand that passes the neck, and there will be a last inhabitant of Laudomia born, a last grain to fall, which is now at the top of the pile, waiting.'

III

In a lecture to writing students, Calvino describes Polo's travels across Kublai Khan's empire as a search for the 'hidden reasons which bring men to live in cities: reasons which remain valid over and above any crisis'. He defines a city as an amalgam of many things: 'Memory, desires, signs of a language; it is a place of exchange, as any textbook of economic history will tell you—only, these exchanges are not just trade in goods, they also involve words, desires, and memories.' What types of exchanges govern the lives of the residents of Laudomia? What drives the commerce that binds the living to the dead and the unborn?

At the start of the chronicles, an unnamed narrator tells the reader that, despite not believing everything Polo has to say, the emperor listens to his tales with greater attention than he devotes to any other of his explorers. The reason for this is the emperor's melancholy disposition and his not infrequent bouts of hypochondria. As far as we can tell, it's not the loss of some precious part of his vast territories that weighs heavily on his outlook. Rather, it's his awareness of a loss that is *still-to-come* and whose hallmark is the creeping inexorability of ruin that shadows even the greatest triumphs. Polo's stories do not assuage the implications of this awareness. Instead, they offer the emperor a glimmer of the very thing that the residents of Laudomia seek from their visits to the dead and the unborn: 'Only in Marco Polo's accounts was Kublai Khan able to discern, through the walls and towers destined to crumble, the tracery of a pattern so subtle it could escape the termites' gnawing.'

The stories told about Adelma and Laudomia transpose the anxiety about time's passing that hangs over the emperor's meditations onto the relationships between the generations that govern the lives of his subjects. Both speak of the need to draw from the course of a lifetime— even one as exalted as that of the Tartar emperor—some pattern that might connect one's existence to those who are no longer and those who are not yet. If pattern is too vague a term, then tradition might be more useful. 'For tradition puts the past in order,' explains Hannah Arendt, 'not just chronologically but first of all systematically in that it separates the positive from the negative, the orthodox from the heretical, and which is obligatory and relevant from the mass of irrelevant or merely interesting opinions and data.' Polo's conversations with the emperor are informed by the realisation that the authority provided by tradition has run its course, leaving his legacy exposed to ruin. This is how we can approach Polo's tales: as 'thought fragments' whose purpose is to render the challenges *and* possibilities that accompany the passing of the generations. The convolutions that define Polo's tales do not reassert the greatness of Kublai Khan's empire or reassure him that things will remain as they are. Rather, they imbue past and future with a sense of possibility.

IV

In the preface to *Between Past and Future*, Arendt locates the feelings of anxiety that we encounter in Polo's tales as indicative of periods in history 'when not only the later historians but the actors and witnesses, the living themselves, become aware of an interval in time which is altogether determined by things that are no longer and by things that are not yet.' Almost immediately, she adds that these intervals are not merely historical periods. They are also constitutive of thinking itself: 'It may well be the region of the spirit or, rather, the path paved by thinking, this small track of non-time which the activity of thought beats within the space-time of mortal men and into which the trains of thought, remembrance and anticipation, save whatever they touch from the ruin of historical and biographical time.' For Arendt, thinking occurs in the gap between a past that is no longer and a future that is not yet. But its most acute manifestations occur during those periods in the life of an individual or broader culture when the habits of thought that serve as the basis of tradition are deemed no longer fit for purpose. The type of thinking that takes place at this point continues to draw on the twin processes of remembrance and anticipation. But now it does so in a manner that is open-ended and must rely on the presence of others. 'This enlarged way of thinking ... cannot function in strict isolation or solitude,' she writes later in the book. 'It needs the presence of others "in whose place" it must think, whose perspectives it must take into consideration, and without whom it never has the opportunity to operate at all.'

Who are these others? On one level, they are the living: the ones whose responses are part of the conversation of public life. But on another level, they are also the dead and the unborn, the ones we turn to in our struggle to save things from the ruin of biographical and historical time. They too are part of what Arendt describes as 'an anticipated communication with others': a form of communication whose terms and conditions have yet to be determined. 'The trouble, however, is that we seem to be neither equipped nor prepared for this activity of thinking, of settling down in the gap between past and future.'

V

Put too simply, perhaps, the allure of Polo's tales for the emperor lies in their capacity to model a way of thinking in the gap between what is no longer and what is not yet. 'You advance always with your head turned back?' Polo imagines the emperor asking him during a quiet moment in one of their conversations. He responds with his own interpretation of his travels: 'What he sought was always something lying ahead, and even if it was a matter of the past it was a past that changed gradually as he advanced on his journey, because the traveler's past changes according to the route he has followed: not the immediate past, that is, to which each day that goes by adds a day, but the more remote past.' So the past that propels Polo's journeys is a past that, with each step forward, changes face. But not just the past. Each step forward also brings a change in the traveler's future. No longer bound to a past that is fixed and stable, it acquires the status of something open to a range of possible configurations. 'Marco enters a city,' begins the most dizzying of the scenarios that sum up Polo's travels:

> He sees someone in a square living a life or an instant that could be his; he could now be in that man's place, if he had stopped in time, long ago; or if, long ago, at a crossroads, instead of taking one road he had taken the opposite one, and after long wandering he had come to be in the place of that man in that square. By now, from that real or hypothetical past of his, he is

excluded; he cannot stop; he must go on to another city, where another of his pasts awaits him, or something perhaps that had been a possible future of his and is now someone else's present.

In this scenario, past and future are the interlinked and constantly changing poles of a present that is still-to-be-determined. This counters the feelings of grim inevitability that paralyse the emperor. Of equal importance, it sets the terms for a form of thinking that does not stand apart from the forces of ruination.

The challenges that accompany this form of thinking is the subject of the final conversation between Polo and the emperor. Leafing through an atlas of the cities that constitute his empire, Kublai Khan falls into a familiar despair. 'It's all useless, if the last landing place can only be the infernal city,' he declares, 'and it is there that, in ever-narrowing circles, the current is drawing us.' In response, Polo insists that the infernal city is not up ahead. Rather, it is here, already, 'the inferno where we live every day, that we form by being together'. He outlines two options for the emperor. 'The first is easy for many: accept the inferno and become such a part of it that you can no longer see it. The second is risky and demands constant vigilance and apprehension: seek and learn to recognize who and what, in the midst of the inferno, are not inferno, then make them endure, give them space.'

The challenge in the second option is to give equal weight to two seemingly opposing scenarios: that the inferno is part of human existence, and that, in the midst of the inferno, we can still identify who and what are not inferno. Vigilance and apprehension cannot forestall life's wearing away and depletion. Instead, they provide the ground for a type of thinking that maintains the past as still-to-be-thought. This is why, when Kublai Khan leafs through the pages of his atlas, he is able to peruse maps not only of the cities that currently exist or that have crumbled into ruins. He is also able to discern the outlines of cities 'that do not yet have a form or a name': future cities 'that will exist one day and in whose place now only hares' holes gape'. These as yet unnamed cities are where we can glean the first stirrings of a past that has yet to come into view.

VI

In an essay on Rainer Maria Rilke's *Duino Elegies*, Arendt considers how these gleanings manifest at the level of the senses. She quotes from the ninth elegy: 'More than ever / the Things that we might experience are vanishing.' The poet's task is to use language to effect a form of rescue in which preservation from destruction coincides with a process of transformation. The exigency driving this endeavour is drawn from the perishability of things, as well as their capacity to act as intermediaries for an engagement with what Rilke refers to as the 'other realm'. In identifying how this engagement operates, Arendt pairs the imperative for speech with a type of listening that doubles as an activity of beseeching. 'A beseeching of this kind does not presuppose the presence of the responding voice; nor does the beseeching of the prayer with which it is actually identical,' she writes. Independent of the responder's presence, this state of 'being-in-hearing', as Arendt calls it, 'pays no attention to whether its beseeching may be heard'. It maintains the possibility of a relationship to an other whose responses are still-to-come. Again, the form of communication conjured here is one which remains anticipated. We pursue it 'with our ears'.

VII

This brings us to the most mysterious of the infernal cities described in Polo's chronicles: Argia. The mystery that surrounds this city is due both to the brevity of the account provided—just two short paragraphs—and the city's subterranean nature. 'What makes Argia different from other cities is that it has earth instead of air,' Polo tells us. 'The streets are completely filled with dirt, clay packs the rooms to the ceiling, on every stair another stairway is set in negative, over the roofs of the houses hang layers of rocky terrain like skies with clouds.' Judging from Polo's account, it is impossible to know how the inhabitants of Argia move about their city or the type of commerce that governs its economy. The surprising thing is that, despite this obscurity, the subterranean city attracts its share of above-ground visitors. The nature of this attraction is never explained. Instead, the story closes with a piece of advice for anyone planning to visit: 'At night, putting your ear to the ground, you can sometimes hear a door slam.'

The connection between the scenario sketched in Polo's account of Argia and the traffic of Laudomia's residents to the dead and the unborn is unmistakable. Both are about the transactions that link the living to the dead and the unborn. Both affirm that human life is lived in proximity to the dead and the unborn. But whereas Laudomia's residents are able to decipher their own names on the stone slabs or picture the unborn as grains of dust floating before them, visitors to Argia must fall back on something more tenuous: a listening that is directed at the earth, its perishability and status as a place of residence; a listening that hovers above the inferno in a state of vigilance and apprehension.

Coda

Like the infernal cities described in Polo's chronicles, the photographs that move us ask that we listen to the murmurings that connect the living to the dead and the unborn. What is that we hear when we listen to these murmurings? Aspirations, intentions, second thoughts, regrets ... the realisation that what had once seemed essential now appears otherwise. The compulsion to attend to these murmurings stems from what we know of the lives represented, as well as what remains secret, the phantoms they have bequeathed to us. Photographs situate all this in the context of what Rilke refers to as 'onceness': 'Once for each thing. Just *once*; no more. And we too, / just once. And never again. But to have been / this once, completely, even if only once: / to have been at one with the earth, seems beyond undoing.' The obligation that Rilke lays at the poet's feet echoes the challenge that Polo describes in his final conversation with the emperor: to give equal weight to the contingency and the irrevocability of all living things. To regard onceness not as the mark of life's limitations, but as the spur for a form of thinking that straddles the uncertain space between a past that is no longer and a future that is not yet.

This obligation is also what the photograph of the four travellers at the start of this book asks of us. *To think*. No doubt, this would be the point in Polo's chronicles when the emperor rises from his seat and, turning his back on the Venetian traveller, declares in undisguised exasperation: *'To what end?'* The conviction that guides this thinking—*its hope*—is that, by lingering in the gap between past and future, we might identify something other than the unceasing process of ruination that bedevils the emperor. Arendt clarifies what this entails by referring to the work of a pearl diver who plumbs the depths of the sea 'not to excavate the bottom and bring it to light but to pry loose the rich and the strange, the pearls and the coral in the depths, and to carry them to the surface'. The goal of the thinker operates in an analogous fashion: not to resuscitate the past, but to extricate from the images that give it shape and depth something new. 'The process of decay is at the same time a process of crystallization,' she adds, 'that in the depth of the sea, into which sinks and is dissolved what once was alive, some things "suffer a sea-change" and survive in a new crystallized forms and shapes that remain immune to the elements, as though they waited only for the pearl diver who one day will come down to them and bring them up into the world of the living.'

This image captures the tension between survival and transformation, preservation and appropriation, that defines the relationship to our forebears. Let's call this tension writing. A writing that identifies who and what in the midst of the inferno are not inferno. A writing that lends an ear to the murmurings that bind us to photographs but, more often than not, makes do with the ringing sound of a door slamming shut. A writing that is able to glean from the buried layers of all the cities visited in the course of a lifetime something that carries with it the directness of a request. The request is simple: *Keep going. There is still much more to be said.*

'I am not writing to say that I have nothing to say,' Georges Perec observes about the gaps that constitute his account of his parents' lives. 'I write because we lived together, because I was one amongst them, a shadow amongst their shadows, a body close to their bodies. I write because they left in me their indelible mark, whose trace is writing; their memory is dead in writing; writing is the memory of their death and the assertion of my life.' He's right, of course. But maybe the reverse is also true: writing as the memory of our death and the assertion of their life—or at least, its unfinishedness.

Notes

No Longer and Not Yet

The idea of the musicality of the photograph is drawn from Tina M. Campt's work on the Dyche photographic archive in *Image Matters: Archive, Photography, and the African Diaspora in Europe* (Durham and London: Durham University Press, 2012). Campt draws extensively on Fred Moten's *In the Break: The Aesthetics of the Black Radical Tradition* (Minneapolis: University of Minnesota Press, 2003).

John Berger, *Understanding a Photograph* (London: Penguin Books, 2013).

Anne Carson, *Economy of the Unlost* (Princeton: Princeton University Press, 1999).

Hannah Arendt, 'No Longer and Not Yet', in *Reflections on Literature and Culture*, edited and introduced by Susannah Young-ah Gottlieb (Stanford: Stanford University Press, 2007).

1. The Bouquet

Philip Roth, *Patrimony: A True Story* (London: Vintage, 1991).

Philip Roth, 'Patrimony', in *Why Write? Collected Nonfiction 1960–2013* (New York: Library of America, 2017).

Roland Barthes, *Camera Lucida: Reflections on Photography* (New York: Hill and Wang, 1980).

Hannah Arendt, 'The Crisis in Education', in *Between Past and Future: Eight Exercises in Political Thought* (New York: Penguin Books, 2006).

Arendt, 'No Longer and Not Yet'.

Annie Ernaux, *A Woman's Story*, translated by Tanya Leslie (New York: Seven Stories Press, 2003).

2. Pacific Park

Bruce Mackenzie, *Design with Landscape* (Sydney: Bruce Mackenzie Design, 2011).

Italo Calvino, *Invisible Cities*, translated by William Weaver (London: Vintage Books, 1997).

3. Moments of Choice

Masha Gessen, 'To Be, or Not to Be', *New York Review of Books*, 65, 2 (8–21 February 2018). In this published lecture, Gessen attributes the idea of the parallel life to the writer and artist Svetlana Boym.

4. The Keys to the House

Antigone Kefala, *Conversations with Mother*, in *Summer Visit: Three Novellas* (Sydney: Giramondo Publishing, 2002).

John Berger, *The Shape of a Pocket* (London: Bloomsbury, 2001).

Siegfried Kracauer, *Theory of Film: The Redemption of Physical Reality* (Princeton: Princeton University Press, 1997). The quote from Kracauer is drawn from Miriam Bratu Hansen's discussion of the writer's unpublished notebooks in her introduction.

George Kouvaros, *Awakening the Eye: Robert Frank's American Cinema* (Minneapolis: University of Minnesota Press, 2015).

Philippe Dubois, 'Video Thinks What Cinema Creates: Notes on Jean-Luc Godard's Work in Video and Television', in *Jean-Luc Godard: Son + Image, 1974–1991*, edited by Raymond Bellour with Mary Lea Bandy (New York: Museum of Modern Art, 1992).

John Berger, *And Our Faces, My Heart, Brief as Photos* (New York: Vintage International, 1991).

Virginia Woolf, 'The Cinema', in *Selected Essays* (Oxford: Oxford University Press, 2008).

Jean-Luc Godard and Anne-Marie Miéville, *The Old Place* (Paris: POL, 2000). Quoted in Antoine de Baecque, *Camera Historica: The Century in Cinema* (New York: Columbia University Press, 2012).

Vinciane Despret, 'Afterword: It Is an Entire World that Has Disappeared', in *Extinction Studies: Stories of Time, Death, and Generations*, edited by

Deborah Bird Rose, Thom Van Dooren and Matthew Chrulew (New York: Columbia University Press, 2017).

5. The Phantom's Call

Víctor Erice, 'Writing Cinema, Thinking Cinema ...', in *The Cinema of Víctor Erice: An Open Window*, edited by Linda C. Ehrlich (Lanham, Maryland: Scarecrow Press, 2007).

Nicolas Abraham, 'Notes on the Phantom: A Complement to Freud's Metapsychology', translated by Nicholas Rand, *Critical Inquiry*, 13, 2 (Winter 1987).

Giorgio Agamben, 'The Last Chapter in the History of the World', in *Nudities*, translated by David Kishik and Stefan Pedatella (Stanford: Stanford University Press, 2011).

Víctor Erice, *The Footprints of a Spirit*, bonus feature included in *The Spirit of the Beehive*, Special Edition Double-Disc Set, Criterion Collection, 2006.

Víctor Erice, 'Can You See Now? (Puedes ver ahora?): A Detailed Commentary about a Sequence in *City Lights*', in *The Cinema of Víctor Erice*. The role played by unspoken memories in binding the child to the experience of cinema is compellingly explored in the video essay *Haunted Memory: the Cinema of Víctor Erice*, Cristina Álvarez López and Adrian Martin, 2016. Available at https://www.youtube.com/watch?v=iTuVd7Ygoiw

Gilberto Perez, *The Material Ghost: Films and Their Medium* (Baltimore: Johns Hopkins University Press, 1998).

Mar Diestro-Dópido, 'My Father the Hero', in the booklet accompanying *El Sur (The South)*, Dual Format Blu-Ray/DVD Edition, BFI, 2017.

6. 'Together with Them We Are Also Alone'

James Agee, 'Knoxville: Summer 1915', in *Let Us Now Praise Famous Men, A Death in the Family and Shorter Fiction* (New York: Library of America, 2005).

Richard Ford, *Between Them: Remembering My Parents* (London: Bloomsbury, 2017).

Richard Ford, *Wildlife* (London: Collins Harvill, 1990).

Emmanuel Levinas, *Totality and Infinity: An Essay on Exteriority*, translated by Alphonso Lingis (Pittsburgh: Duquesne University Press, 1961).

W. H. Auden, 'Musée des Beaux Arts', in *Selected Poems* (New York: Vintage Books, 1979).

7. 'A Poor and Precious Secret'

Patrick Modiano, *Dora Bruder*, translated by Joanna Kilmartin (Berkeley: University of California Press, 1999).

Walter Benjamin, 'On the Concept of History', in *Selected Writings*, Volume 4: 1938–1940, translated by Edmund Jephcott et al. (Cambridge, Massachusetts: Belknap Press of Harvard University Press, 2003).

André Bazin, 'The Ontology of the Photographic Image', in *What Is Cinema?* (Berkeley and Los Angeles: University of California Press, 1967).

Patrick Modiano, *Dora Bruder* (Paris: Editions Gallimard, 1997). 'On oubliait, le temps d'une séance, la guerre et les menaces du dehors. Dans l'obscurité d'une salle de cinéma, on était serrés les uns contre les autres, à suivre le flot des images de l'écran, et plus rien ne pouvait arriver.' In his account of this passage, Sven-Erik Rose claims that the use of the French 'on', rendered in Joanna Kilmartin's translation as 'you', 'allows the narrator to include himself in the phenomenon he describes. He, too, is borne away by the flow of images and in his own way pulled into the experimental space of the film, where he commingles briefly with its historical viewers.' Sven-Erik Rose, 'Remembering Dora Bruder: Patrick Modiano's Surrealist Encounter with the Postmemorial Archive,' *Postmodern Culture*, 18, 2 (January 2008).

Susan Weiner, 'Dora Bruder and the Longue Durée', *Studies in 20th and 21st Century Literature*, 31, 2 (2007).

Jacques Derrida, *Memoires for Paul de Man*, revised edition (New York: Columbia University Press, 1989).

Jean Louis Schefer, *The Ordinary Man of Cinema*, translated by Max Cavitch, Paul Grant and Noura Wedell (New York: Semiotext(e), 2016).

Patrick Modiano, *Afterimage*, in *Suspended Sentences: Three Novellas*, translated by Mark Polizzotti (New Haven: Yale University Press, 2014).

8. 'A Light from Before'

Annie Ernaux, *The Years*, translated by Alison L. Strayer (London: Fitzcarraldo Editions, 2018).

Bazin, 'The Ontology of the Photographic Image'.

Annie Ernaux, *A Man's Place*, translated by Tanya Leslie (London: Fitzcarraldo Editions, 2021).

Arendt, 'Preface: The Gap Between Past and Future', in *Between Past and Future*.

Ernaux, *A Woman's Story*.

Annie Ernaux, *I Remain in Darkness*, translated by Tanya Leslie (New York: Seven Stories Press, 2011).

9. As If It Were for the Last Time

Wim Wenders, *Pictures from the Surface of the Earth* (Munich: Schirmer Art Books, 2003).

Wim Wenders, 'Wim Wenders in Conversation with Alain Bergala', in *Written in the West* (New York: teNeues Publishing, 2000).

Wim Wenders, 'The Men in the Rodeo Arena: Lusty', in *On Film: Essays and Conversations*, translated by Michael Hofmann (London: Faber and Faber, 2001).

Walker Evans, quoted in Jerry L. Thompson, *Walker Evans at Work* (New York: Harper and Row, 1982).

Geoff Dyer, *The Ongoing Moment* (London: Little Brown, 2005).

Miriam Bratu Hansen, Introduction, in Kracauer, *Theory of Film*.

Gerhard Richter, *Afterness: Figures of Following in Modern Thought and Aesthetics* (New York: Columbia University Press, 2011).

Wenders, *Pictures from the Surface of the Earth*.

Wim Wenders, *Journey to Onomichi* (Munich: Schirmer/Mosel, 2010).

Thomas Elsaesser, 'Spectators of Life: Time, Place, and Self in the Films of Wim Wenders', in *The Cinema of Wim Wenders: Image, Narrative and the Postmodern Condition*, edited by Roger F. Cook and Gerd Gemünden (Detroit, Michigan: Wayne State University Press, 1997).

Walter Benjamin, 'The Image of Proust', in *Illuminations: Essays and Reflections*, edited and introduced by Hannah Arendt, translated by Harry Zohn (Suffolk: Fontana, 1982).

Wim Wenders, 'Impossible Stories', in *The Cinema of Wim Wenders*.

Lee Strasberg, 'A Dream of Passion: The Development of the Method', in *Star Texts: Image and Performance in Film and Television*, edited by Jeremy Butler (Detroit: Wayne State University Press, 1991).

Walter Benjamin, 'The Formula in Which the Dialectical Structure of Film Finds Expression', in *Selected Writings*, Volume 3, 1935–1938, translated by Edmund Jephcott et al. (Cambridge, Massachusetts: Belknap Press of Harvard University Press, 2002).

10. The Work of Mourning

Sigmund Freud, 'Mourning and Melancholia', in *The Standard Edition of the Complete Psychological Works of Sigmund Freud*, translated by James Strachey, in collaboration with Anna Freud, assisted by Alix Strachey and Alan Tyson, Volume XIV (1914–1916), On the History of the Psycho-Analytic Movement, Papers on Metapsychology and Other Works (London: Hogarth Press and the Institute of Psycho-Analysis, 1957).

Roland Barthes, *Mourning Diary*, translated and with an afterword by Richard Howard (New York: Hill and Wang, 2010).

Georgia Metaxas's artist statement can be found at georgiametaxas.com/frameset.htm

James Agee, Introduction, in Walker Evans, *Many Are Called* (New Haven and London: Yale University Press, 2004).

Jean-Luc Nancy, *The Inoperative Community*, edited by Peter Connor, translated by Peter Connor, Lisa Garbus, Michael Holland and Simona Sawhney (Minneapolis: University of Minnesota Press, 1991).

Walter Benjamin, 'Little History of Photography', in *Selected Writings*, Volume 2: 1927–1934, translated by Rodney Livingstone et al. (Cambridge, Massachusetts: Belknap Press of Harvard University Press, 1999).

Denis Diderot, quoted in Michael Fried, *Absorption and Theatricality: Painting and Beholder in the Age of Diderot* (Chicago: Chicago University Press, 1980).

Michael Fried, 'Between Realisms: From Derrida to Manet', *Critical Inquiry*, 21, 1 (1994).

Michael Fried, *Why Photography Matters as Art as Never Before* (New Haven: Yale University Press, 2008). The term 'to-be-seenness' is drawn from this book.

Martin Heidegger, *Being and Time*, translated by John Macquarrie and Edward Robinson (New York: Harper and Row, 1962).

Maurice Blanchot, *The Unavowable Community*, translated by Pierre Joris (New York: Station Hill Press, 1988).

Barthes, *Camera Lucida*.

Cities and the Dead

The transactional nature of the relationship between the living and the dead is central to Anne Carson's discussion of the history and nature of epitaphs in *Economy of the Unlost*.

Italo Calvino, 'Italo Calvino on *Invisible Cities*', *Columbia: a Journal of Literature and Art* (Spring/Summer 1983).

Arendt's remarks on tradition can be found in her introduction to Benjamin's *Illuminations*. The term 'thought fragments' is drawn from the same source.

Arendt, 'Preface: The Gap Between Past and Future', in *Between Past and Future*.

Hannah Arendt and Günther Stern, 'Rilke's *Duino Elegies*', in *Reflections on Literature and Culture*.

Rainer Maria Rilke, *Duino Elegies*, in *The Selected Poetry of Rainer Maria Rilke*, edited and translated by Stephen Mitchell (New York: Random House, 1982). The lines concerning 'onceness' appear in the Ninth Elegy.

Coda

Arendt's reflections on the work of the pearl diver appear in her introduction to Benjamin's *Illuminations*.

Georges Perec, *W or the Memory of Childhood* (London: Collins Harvill, 1989).

Acknowledgements

I am grateful to the editors of *Southerly*, *Sydney Review of Books*, *Movie*, *Textual Practice* and *New German Critique* for the opportunity to air the ideas that, slowly, slowly, led to this book. Roanna Gonsalves read a draft of the manuscript and provided valuable feedback. I also benefitted from the feedback provided by John Hughes and Angela Rockel. Thank you Terri-ann White for believing in the value of these essays.

In its themes and governing questions, *Patrimonies* is an extension of my previous publication: *The Old Greeks: Photography, Cinema, Migration*. In this book, I pay tribute to the members of my family, living and dead, whose labour, dedication and sacrifices made its writing possible. Finding ways to place this patrimony at the centre of my writing—rather than as an afterthought—remains an overriding concern. The connection between these books also explains why, in some of the more directly autobiographical passages, I have returned to incidents, recollections and even images that appear in the earlier book. I hope that the discomfort this might cause is compensated by the opportunity to think again about the debts and obligations that form the foundation of my good fortune. At the very least, it affirms their on-going nature.

About Upswell

Upswell Publishing was established in 2021 by Terri-ann White as a not-for-profit press. A perceived gap in the market for distinctive literary works in fiction, poetry and narrative non-fiction was the motivation. In her years as a bookseller, writer and then publisher, Terri-ann has maintained a watch on literary books and the way they insinuate themselves into a cultural space and are then located within our literary and cultural inheritance. She is interested in making books to last: books with the potential to still be noticed, and noted, after decades and thus be ripe to influence new literary histories.

About this typeface

Book designer Becky Chilcott chose Foundry Origin not only as a strong, carefully considered, and dependable typeface, but also to honour her late friend and mentor, type designer Freda Sack, who oversaw the project. Designed by Freda's long-standing colleague, Stuart de Rozario, much like Upswell Publishing, Foundry Origin was created out of the desire to say something new.

www.ingramcontent.com/pod-product-compliance
Lightning Source LLC
Chambersburg PA
CBHW030112170426
43198CB00009B/591